The Rooted Life

The Rooted Life

Tree Wisdom for Living the Christian Life

Mark Mah

RESOURCE *Publications* • Eugene, Oregon

THE ROOTED LIFE
Tree Wisdom for Living the Christian Life

Copyright © 2019 Mark Mah. All rights reserved. Except for brief quotations in critical publications or reviews, no part of this book may be reproduced in any manner without prior written permission from the publisher. Write: Permissions, Wipf and Stock Publishers, 199 W. 8th Ave., Suite 3, Eugene, OR 97401.

Resource Publications
An Imprint of Wipf and Stock Publishers
199 W. 8th Ave., Suite 3
Eugene, OR 97401

www.wipfandstock.com

PAPERBACK ISBN: 978-1-5326-8995-6
HARDCOVER ISBN: 978-1-5326-8996-3
EBOOK ISBN: 978-1-5326-8997-0

Manufactured in the U.S.A.   MAY 28, 2019

For all my students who taught me
how to be a better teacher.

They will be called oaks of righteousness,
a planting of the Lord for the display of his splendor.

—Isaiah 61:3

He is like a tree planted by streams of water,
which yields its fruit in season and whose leaf does
not wither. Whatever he does prospers.

—Psalm 1:3

Contents

1. People are like Trees / 1
2. The Rooted Life / 14
3. The Communal Life / 27
4. The Sacrificial Life / 41
5. The Reviewed Life / 54
6. The Abiding Life / 67
7. The Rejuvenated Life / 81
8. The Grateful Life / 93
9. The Delayed Life / 106
10. The Cross-bearing Christian / 119

Questions for Personal Reflection and Group Discussion / 135
Bibliography / 141

1

People are like Trees

When we have learned how to listen to trees,
then the brevity and the quickness
and the childlike hastiness of our thoughts
achieve an incomparable joy.

—Hermann Hesse

Comparing People to Trees

THE JEWS CELEBRATE THE New Year for Trees on the 15th of Shevat. This is based on the Torah that compares a person to a tree in a field (Deut 20:19). On this day children are given a bag filled with raisins, dates, and carob. They also collect money to plant trees in Israel. Trees play an important part in people's lives and are greatly appreciated because of the arid climate in Israel. Buildings made of wood were highly valued and considered luxurious in biblical times. The interior of the temple was paneled with cedar and pine wood. Doors were made of olive wood. Abraham's planting of a tamarisk tree in Beersheba and the great trees of Mamre where he pitched his tent deserved mention in Scripture

(Gen 18:1; 21:33). Planting trees holds symbolic meaning for the people of Israel. A tree is planted to commemorate the birth of a child. Both are miracles of God's creation: a young tree that grows from a seed and a newborn that grows from the seed planted in the mother's womb. The child, like the roots of a tree that sink deep into the ground for strength and growth, will grow up being nourished by drawing from the traditional roots of family and heritage. Typically for a male child, a cedar tree is planted and for the female child, a cypress tree is planted. Hopefully, the young boy will grow up to have the strength of a cedar tree and the girl will grow up as bright and fragrant as a cypress tree.

The Bible, in some places, compares a person to a tree. A blessed man, according to the psalmist, is like a tree planted by streams of water (Ps 1:3). In the Song of Songs, the beloved compares her lover to an apple tree: "Like an apple tree among the trees of the forest is my lover among the young men. I delight to sit in his shade and his fruit is sweet to my taste" (Song 2:3). Once, Jesus healed a blind man at Bethsaida. Jesus, after spitting on the blind man's eyes and putting his hands on him, asked whether he saw anything. He replied by saying that he saw people were like trees walking around (Mark 8:23–4).

Our Connection with Trees

It is not surprising for people to compare themselves to trees. A tree is a sign of strength, stability, growth, and usefulness. We are surrounded by trees all the time. They look benign and do not threaten our existence. Humans can coexist well with trees. Trees give us a sense of security and delight. We take shelter under them to shield us from the rain or sun. We climb trees to get a better view from the top. The rustling of leaves on a windy day has a soothing effect on our nerves. The changing colors of leaves and fruits is a delight to the eyes. We use them to satisfy our needs for food, wood, and shade. Trees do not complain or talk back at us. Perhaps we feel a strong connection with trees because we share some similar physical appearances with them. Trees are rooted to the ground, have a body made of a trunk and branches, and crowned with leaves at the top. We stand upright like a rooted tree, have an upright body with limbs, and a crown of hair on top of our heads.

We change physically when we age. Our skin gets wrinkled, age spots appear on our arms and faces, the hair starts to drop and gets thinner, the body is not getting taller but wider at the waist. We begin to lose our body mass and our muscles get weaker. Trees also have similar changes when they age. When trees age, their "skin" or bark is no longer smooth but wrinkled and rough. Moss and algae appear on the branches or at the branch forks. They stop growing taller. This is due to the inability of the roots and vascular system to pump water and nutrients to the top. The pressure to exert is too much for the old trees. Instead, they grow wider. The energy level is slowly diminishing leading to the loss of body mass. The storms sweep the dead twigs away and are not replaced by new shoots. The crown gets thinner with each stormy weather due to the disappearance of the twigs and branches at the top.[1]

Childhood Memories

I think our association with trees stems from our childhood days. I can still remember those times when we had to climb a tree in order to view a movie for free. Television (the black and white version) was still a luxurious household item in those days. Few people owned a television set at home. My house was near to an entertainment park. The park was our only entertainment outlet. In the park was a theater. We could buy a ticket to enter the theater. If we were already in the park, we could go in and watch a movie by a different entrance without a ticket. Those without tickets would be standing throughout the screening of the movie. The seated and standing sections of the theater were separated by a wired fence. We had to pay an entrance fee to enter the park. The park was located next to a school and a wall separated them. We had to climb

---

1. Wohlleben, *The Hidden Life of Trees*, 65–66.

over a high wall to enter the park without paying the entrance fee. On the school grounds was a tree that grew next to the wall. That was our secret entrance to the park. We climbed the tree to get to the wall in order to jump over it. As children, we did not mind the risks that we took. We just enjoyed the thrill of climbing, jumping, and watching movies for free!

We also climbed trees to get a better view or to escape from the neighbor's crazy dog. We swung on tree branches and shook the leaves for fun. We carved words on tree barks to mark our presence or to express an intimate passion. Tree stories captured our imagination. *Jack and the Beanstalk* was one of my favorites. I read the story of the *Giving Tree* by Shel Silverstein with appreciation and awe. Children love to stay away from the grownups and do their own things. We dreamed of having a tree house. It would just be the hiding place for our neighborhood gang to meet and to have a little privacy.

A Tree is like a Mirror

If people are like trees then we can learn something about ourselves by looking at trees. "A tree is like a mirror that reflects my best self," writes Rochel Holzkenner.[2] Belden Lane, a professor at Saint Louis University, recalls, in *Ravished by Beauty*, how he got acquainted with a tall Eastern Cottonwood. The tree was located in a park just across the street from his home. Part of the tree was torn down during a severe windstorm. A huge gaping hole, caused by the storm, was seen on one side of the big tree. Lane was there when Park Service workers cut and cleared the fallen parts. This chance meeting with the tree was providential. At that time he also experienced breakage due to his mother's Alzheimer and cancer. He was the only child and had to bear the grief alone. From that time on, Lane shared with the tree his worries and future concerns. He called this tree "Grandfather".

---

2. Holzkenner, "Roots of Resilience" No page.

We share a lot together, Grandfather and I. He knew pain and relinquishment, and taught me much about relationship, about waiting and letting go, about detachment that make love possible . . . He tells me not to worry or rush around so much. "Everything you really need will come to you," he says. Only a creature that cannot move, who has to trust and wait, can say that with genuine persuasiveness.[3]

Hermann Hesse believes that we have a lot to learn from trees if we care to listen to them. Trees, to him, are the most penetrating preachers. He compares a beautiful strong tree to solitary figures like Beethoven and Nietzsche whose strength lied in being themselves and were able to chart their own paths in life. Trees, being immobile, have their own ways to deal with outside threats. They cannot run away to avoid trouble but are able to overcome with great patience and strong resilience against all kinds of adversaries. Hermann Hesse, German novelist and painter, in *Trees: Reflections and Poems* writes:

> Trees are sanctuaries. Whoever knows how to speak to them, whoever knows how to listen to them, can learn the truth. They do not preach learning and precepts, they preach, undeterred by particulars, the ancient law of life.[4]

We are like Sheep

This sheep metaphor used widely in Scripture gives us a better understanding of the character and behavior of God's people. Like sheep, we can easily go astray (Isa 53:6). Sheep are not the smartest of animals. They can get lost if they do not follow the shepherd closely (John 10:4). Sheep, by nature, are timid and easily get distressed and fearful. They need more care and protection than other animals. The shepherd's rod is to fence off any predators that attack the sheep. The staff is to direct the sheep to stay close to the flock

---

3. Lane, *Ravished by Beauty*, 129.

4. Popova, "Hermann Hesse on What Trees Teach Us about Belonging and Life."

(Ps 23:4). Sheep need to rest periodically. If not, they will get sick due to exhaustion. They will not lie down and rest if they harbor fears. These fears can be caused by several factors: friction within members of the flock, parasites or flies that torment the sheep, and hunger that causes them to look for food.[5] Only the shepherd, who knows his sheep well, can make them lie down and rest in green pastures (John 10:14; Ps 23:2). Sheep will drink from any water source. The shepherd will lead them to get clean, pure water to quench their thirst. Unclean water will bring bad health for the sheep due to intestinal parasites.[6]

The sheep metaphor is helping us to understand and appreciate not only who we are but also who God is to his people, how he sees his people, and what is required of them. In a similar vein, the tree metaphor in this book helps us to gain insights into the Christian life. Most of us have seen sheep. Not many of us have the opportunity to get close to a sheep. Trees are different. They are everywhere. We get close to them all the time. We love trees and share a close affinity with them.

The Tree Metaphor

The tree metaphor captures our imagination precisely because of our childhood memories and association with trees. Metaphorical language is used widely in Scripture. Embedded in the stories of Jesus were metaphors that easily stirred the imagination and captured the attention of the listeners. No wonder people found Jesus to be an excellent teacher. Unlike the Pharisees who liked to use precise language in order to define, control, regulate and defend, Jesus spoke in parables. Parables are narrated metaphors. They are made-up stories placed in the context of the familiar and factual. They carry over or across something known to something unknown. They act as a link between the visible and the invisible. A metaphor is a bridge that links our sense experience with our

---

5. Keller, *A Shepherd Looks at Psalm 23*, 35.
6. Keller, *A Shepherd Looks at Psalm 23*, 50.

faith experience. It uses the tangible to explain the intangible. The psalmist uses metaphorical language to address his God. God, in his mind, is powerful and able to deliver him from his troubles when he addresses God as a rock, shield, and horn.

> My God is my rock, in whom I take refuge. He is my shield and the horn of my salvation, my stronghold. I call to the Lord who is worthy of praise, and I am saved from my enemies (Ps 18:2–3).

I will use the tree metaphor, throughout this book, to help us understand and appreciate the Christian life. There are amazing things we can learn from trees. I will consider, metaphorically, the different parts of a tree: its roots, trunk, branches, leaves, and seeds. Each part of the tree gives valuable insights into the Christian life. The roots, which are invisible to the naked eye, refer to the inner life of the Christian. The root system shared among trees refers to the need to live in community by helping each other. The trunk, which is wood and has rings in it, points to the need for Christians to live sacrificially and to review their lives periodically. The branches instruct Christians to draw strength from Christ by abiding in him. Without Christ, they can do nothing. The leaves teach Christians to seek refreshment and rejuvenation of their souls when they enter a dry patch in their lives. The leaves that turn the sun's energy into sugars point to God as the source of our existence and sustenance. This thought reminds them to be always thankful and not to take things for granted. The seed that falls to the ground teaches Christians to stay put and wait on God. It also teaches them to learn to die to the false self in order to gain a foothold in their spiritual lives.

The Rooted Life

Chapter 2 highlights the importance of taking charge of the inner life. We learn about this by observing the roots of trees. The health and well-being of a tree lie in its roots. We seldom take notice of the roots because they are not visible, hidden underneath the soil. More attention and care are given to what is above ground: the body of the tree which comprises of the trunk, branches, and leaves. The fruits that the tree produces will certainly capture our notice. The roots that nourish the tree with water and minerals will make the tree fruitful. The wise man agrees when he says, "The root of the righteous flourishes" (Prov 12:12). He does not say that it is the body of the tree that produces fruit. The biographies of godly men and women normally celebrate the fruit of their labors in terms of their achievements in the name of Christ.[7] They seldom give attention to their roots. No mention is made about the struggles they went through in order to sink their roots deep into the soil. They patiently suffered pain and loss, over a period of watchful waiting, before they could see the fruits in their labors. We need to take care of the inner life before the outer life can flourish. Most of us are in a haste to produce fruit even though the roots are shallow and not yet strong. In the story of the Parable of the Sower, the seed that is planted on rocky soil springs up quickly. The young plant, because of the shallow soil and has not taken root in it, is easily scorched by the strong sun (Matt 13:6). The outer life is an outflow or expression of the inner life. Unless we spend time cultivating our inner being, our outer life may bear fruit for a while but it will not last.

The Communal Life

We will look at the communal life of the Christian in chapter 3. Valuable lessons are gained by observing the root system of trees. Trees, though standing alone, are connected to each other through their root system. They help each other through the exchange of much-needed nutrients. It is observed that some tree stumps have green plants growing on them. A tree stump cannot survive by itself because photosynthesis cannot occur without leaves. Leaves draw water from the roots which is a necessary component for photosynthesis to take place. With water, carbon dioxide, and

---

7. Tozer, *The Root of the Righteous*, 9–10.

sunlight, the tree is able to produce sugars. The sugars are broken down into energy. Trees need sugars for growth and repairs. The reason a tree stump is able to survive, despite the lack of photosynthesis, is because other trees in the vicinity are feeding the stump through the root system. Trees also help one another to create a micro-climatic ecosystem. The ecosystem moderates the local temperatures, stores moisture, and generates humidity. A tree, by itself, is not able to generate a consistent local climate conducive for growth and sustenance. Trees by helping one another receive help themselves. The need for a communal life is obvious for Christians. They are to love and bear one another's burdens (Gal 6:3). Christians, like trees, cannot stand alone and survive spiritually. We are to show concern for one another as members of Christ's body (1 Cor 12:25).

The Sacrificial Life

Chapter 4 calls on us to live sacrificially for God. We learn this by observing the trunk of the tree. We value the trunk for its wood. It is difficult to imagine a world without wood. Wood is nature's most versatile material. We use wood for all kinds of things because it can be easily cut, planed, hollowed, and crafted into all kinds of shapes and sizes. The tree, because of its usefulness, has to sacrifice its wood for use by us. The tree goes through all kinds of physical dismembering in order to produce wood. The tree is fell and the trunk is separated from its roots and crown. The branches are stripped clean and the bark removed. The trunk, which has the most biomass, is ready to be cut into planks and blocks for commercial use. Shel Silverstein's classic tale of *The Giving Tree* is a fine example of how the tree gives its life to be cut and used. Paul calls on us not only to believe in Christ but also to suffer for him as well (Phil 1:29).

The Reviewed Life

Chapter 5 stresses on the need to review our lives before God. Cutting a trunk across its length reveals its rings. The rings record the history of a tree. They reveal to us the different seasons and environmental conditions the tree encountered through its lifespan. There were years when the tree endured drought, fire, and scarcity. There was little growth. There were also years of abundant sunlight and rain to spur growth. Natural calamities endured by the tree throughout its lifetime are clearly marked on its rings. An enduring tree under severe conditions is stronger, healthier, and can survive longer. People who have weathered life's extremities can testify to this fact. Reviewing the work of God in our lives is like observing the rings in a cut trunk. A time set aside to review and examine the "rings" in our lives will let us know where we have been and where God is leading us. We can then get a glimpse of God's work in us "to will and to act according to his good purpose" (Phil 2:13).

The Abiding Life

Chapter 6 focuses on our need to be anchored in Christ. The branches of trees have a lot to teach us about remaining in Christ (John 15:4). Branches are joined to a solid trunk. The trunk gives strength to the branches by nurturing and anchoring them. The branches need to be properly anchored to the trunk in order to support the leaves that form the crown of the tree. Leaves are not heavy. They become heavy when they are soaked with rainwater, covered with snow or pummeled with strong winds. The strength of branches is severely tested to the limit due to the increased weight of the leaves. There will be 27 square yards of leaves that form the crowns of trees for every square yard of forest.[8] We often find shelter under a leafy tree when it is raining. We notice that the amount of rain falling under a tree is very much less than rain falling just outside it. Much of the rainwater is intercepted in

---

8. Wohlleben, *The Hidden Life of Trees*, 106

the canopy and very little falls through. The weight of the leaves is heavier by many times due to the water captured on the leaves. This will not cause trouble to the branches if they are properly anchored to the main trunk. Branches that are not properly anchored will break from the trunk during heavy storms. In the Parable of the Vine and Branches, Jesus calls on us to remain (anchored) in his love if we want to bear fruit. A severed or broken branch cannot bear fruit and is useless. "Without me, you can do nothing," Jesus said to his disciples (John 15:5,10).

The Rejuvenated Life

Chapter 7 highlights for us the need to be refreshed and rejuvenated by the Spirit when we face a dry patch in our lives. The leaves of trees can play a critical role in the weather. Leaves not only hold water when it rains but they also release moisture through transpiration into the air to form clouds. Clouds that are formed by evaporation over the sea can only be carried by the wind to a few hundred miles inland. Habitation is only possible on a narrow strip of land that hugs around the coast. Land that is further inland will be dry without clouds. Here is where forests play a critical role to bring water further inland. Through transpiration, water vapor released by the leaves will form clouds that move further inland to release the rain. This process is repeated over and over resulting in downpours as heavy as those in the coastal areas thousands of miles inland.[9] In a forested area, the rain trapped by the leaves does not splash heavily on the soil below resulting in small streams of flowing water. In this way, water is drained away quickly and wasted. Instead, the water is collected and absorbed by the soft soil when it drips slowly to the ground. Water is retained in this manner and the land is refreshed and rejuvenated. We know that water symbolizes the Holy Spirit in the Bible. Jesus says that those who are thirsty should come to him for a drink of the living water and be refreshed (John 7:37-9). As the parched land needs water,

9. Wohlleben, *The Hidden Life of Trees*, 105–6.

so our dry and thirsty souls need the refreshment of the Spirit of God in order for us to remain healthy and growing.

The Grateful Life

In chapter 8, we want to talk about thanking God for he is the source of our existence and sustenance. Leaves play an important role in photosynthesis. Leaves are green in color because they have chlorophyll. Chlorophyll is a photoreceptor that traps the light from the sun and uses its energy to convert carbon dioxide and water into glucose or sugars which is food for the trees. All living things need energy to survive. We get the energy from the food we eat. All the energy we consume comes from the sun if we trace the food chain. Energy from the sun is transferred to the trees and plants through photosynthesis. Trees or plants make sugars that other living things including humans consume. Trees and plants which form the base of the food chain play a critical role in our survival on this planet. Without the sun's energy, nothing can survive on earth. Christians should look to God as the source of their physical and spiritual existence and well-being. Their lives are dependent on him and nothing else. This should keep them humble and thankful at all times.

The Delayed Life

To wait and stay in the place that God has called us is the message of chapter 9. We learn this by knowing the role seeds play in reproduction. Trees are counting on seeds to reproduce themselves. This is usually done by dispersing the seeds away from the parent tree. Some seeds fall to the ground below while others are carried by the wind. Some types of seeds make use of animals, birds or even humans to disperse them. Exploding seed pods force the seeds to shoot into the air for dispersal. Water can also play a role in the dispersal of seeds. Seeds dispersed by water can travel a long distance from the mother tree. The seed will land somewhere. And where it lands, it will stay put in that place. It has no choice of place but has to make use of the existing conditions to survive. As Christians, we are called to wait on God. Waiting will nourish in us the qualities of patience, trust, hope, gentleness, and compassion. It is not easy for us in this quick-fix society to wait thinking it is a waste of time. We rather make things happen than let things happen. Waiting nurtures our soul. There are many examples of people waiting on God in the Bible: Noah waited for the flood to subside; Moses waited for forty years in the wilderness; the father waiting for the prodigal son to return home; the disciples waited for Pentecost to come; the church waiting for the Lord's return.

The Cross-Bearing Life

The self must die in order for us to gain a foothold in our spiritual lives is the message of chapter 10. We learn that seeds that hit the ground will need to rot and die before it can reproduce. The Bible says that "unless a kernel of wheat falls to the ground and dies, it remains only a single seed. But if it dies, it produces many seeds (John 12:24). Death to the false self is part of following Jesus. Jesus said that those who followed him must take up his or her cross. Bearing the cross will lead to the place of death. The false or homemade self is an impediment to our soul. Unless we deal with this strong sense of self in us we will not be able to advance much in our spiritual lives. This false self thrives on security, control, and affection. It is not easy for us to give up on these things that are working well for us. Emptying the self in us will give space for God to work in our lives. The disciplines of solitude and silence will play a key role in the abandonment of the false self.

2

The Rooted Life

"So then, just as you received Christ Jesus as Lord,
continue to live in him,
rooted and built up in him,
strengthened in the faith as you were taught,
and overflowing with thanksgiving"

—COL 2:6-7

The Soul is a Tree

Catherine of Siena, a fourteenth-century saint, began receiving visions from God at the age of six. She cut her hair in protest when pressured to get married by her parents. She became a nun at the age of eighteen and began serving the poor at the age of twenty-one. She established a monastery for women in 1370. After this, she recorded her visions in her book entitled *The Dialogue*.[1] In this book, she described how God used the image of a tree to show her the way a soul should grow.

---

1. Maricle, *Deeply Rooted*, 9–11.

> Now, consider, in the same way, that the soul is a tree existing by love, and that it can live by nothing else than love; and, that if this soul have not in very truth the divine love of perfect charity, she cannot produce the fruit of life, but only death. It is necessary then, that the root of this tree, that is the affection of the soul, should grow . . .[2]

We need a mental map that can guide us in living a transformed life. The tree metaphor used throughout in this book provides such a map. We often think that transformation begins from the outside in terms of what we can or cannot do. Real transformation begins from within ourselves. That is why we begin by looking at the roots of the tree. Roots are the invisible part of the tree. Since they are out of sight, they are also out of mind as well. Roots do not receive our attention because they are invisible. We pay close attention to what is visible: its trunk, branches, leaves, and fruits. This is normal human behavior. When we clean the room, unless we want to do a thorough job, we will not vacuum the underside of the bed or get rid of the dust collected behind the cupboard. We only clean those areas that are visible to the eye. We pay close attention to what is seen than to what is not seen.

An Inside Look

Most Christians desire change in their lives. Growth can be painful and requires time for transformation to take place. Many, who look for instant relief, do not have the patience to take a deeper look into their lives. They also refuse to take an inside look for fear that it will uncover some hidden secrets that lie buried deep inside them (Matt 23:27). Some people avoid going for a medical checkup for the same reason. They fear that the examination may reveal the true state of their health. Christians look for changes on the outside but "real changes require an inside look" according to Larry Crabb, a well-known psychologist and Bible teacher.[3] Many Christians wrongly conceive the idea that the way to a transformed

2. Maricle, *Deeply Rooted*, 127.
3. Crabb, *Inside Out*, 38.

life is to do what Christians ought to do: to pray, read the Word, witness, serve the church, and give offerings and tithes. Some take these responsibilities seriously but find that they have fallen short. They feel guilty for not measuring up.[4] They may live with this guilt for years thinking that something is wrong with them. The root of the problem lies in the neglect of their inner lives. Paul's prayer for us is that we may be strengthened in the inner being through the power of the Spirit (Eph 3:16). Peter reminds us that God is more interested in our inner self than our outward appearance (1 Pet 3:4). We are to guard our hearts for it is the wellspring of life (Prov 4:23).

Real transformation to our character takes place in our inner life. The changes we hope to see in our lives will not take place unless we take an inside look. We need to go down to the "root" of the problem in spiritual transformation. The most important part of the tree is the roots. If the soul is like a tree, then the inner life should be taken seriously. For a tree to grow well, stay healthy, and bearing fruit, it must have good and strong roots. The Sequoia tree is one of the largest and oldest trees in the world. It weighs over a million kilograms, reaches a height of 300 feet, and can live up to 3000 years. This majestic tree owes its height and weight to its roots. The sequoia's root system spreads over an acre wide and is 12–14 feet deep.

Roots Provide Stability

The roots have several functions. One of them is to provide stability for the tree. The trunk will be able to grow straight up if the roots are deep and well spread out. A straight trunk with deep roots will help the tree to weather strong winds. A curved trunk means that the load on the tree caused by the crown is unevenly distributed. This causes stress to the tree and makes it less stable. The footing of the tree on sloppy terrain is less firm and is thrown off balance. The trunk will not be able to grow straight up. Trees on

---

4. Crabb, *Inside Out*, 65.

a slope are more vulnerable to the wind and weather conditions.[5] Similarly, we will be able to overcome and not be overwhelmed by the external forces that are lashing at our souls if our inner lives are firmly rooted in Jesus. James writes that the trials that test our faith will help develop and mature our character provided that we persevere through them. We will no longer be like the man who doubts and is easily blown and tossed by the wind. Such a man, who is not rooted in Jesus, will be double-minded and unstable in all he does (James 1:6-8).

For those Christians who are deeply rooted in Jesus, the outcome of spiritual formation gives life and vitality not only to the spirit and soul but also to the body as well. The parts of the body (tongue, eyes, hands, facial expressions) are consecrated and used as instruments for God. Willard in his article, "Living a Transformed Life" writes:

> The bodies of these people even look different. There is a freshness about them, a kind of quiet strength, and a transparency. They are rested and playful in a bodily strength that is from God. He who raised up Christ Jesus from the dead has given life to their bodies through his Spirit that dwells in them (Rom 8:10–12).[6]

Fending Off Diseases

Another function of roots is to help the tree fend off harmful pathogens in the air and in the soil. The soil around the roots must be biologically active with good microbes. The roots, working with these microbes, will fend off the pathogens by competing with them for nutrients in the soil and feeding on them as well. The roots also produce an enzyme that kills or suppresses the harmful pathogens. Like sin, these pathogens are always present in the vicinity of the tree. The tree can easily get sick if it lacks immunity due to poor roots. Christians who are deeply rooted in Jesus should be able to ward off the diseases that afflict their souls. The diseases afflicting

---

5. Wohlleben, *The Hidden Life of Trees*, 38–41.
6. Willard, *Renewing the Christian Mind*, 47.

our spiritual lives are identified traditionally as the eight "deadly" sins or thoughts. These thoughts will stir up the unruly passions in us to sin against God if we do not master them. These thoughts are universally experienced by most people all the time. They are considered deadly not because they are like the sins of murder or theft but because they predispose us to sin. These passions, when aroused by these thoughts, will distract us from spiritual matters and weaken our faith. According to Evagrius, a fourth-century monastic scholar, these are the eight deadly thoughts: gluttony, lust, greed, sadness, anger, apathy, vainglory, and pride. The list was later shortened to seven when vainglory was combined with pride as one sin instead of two.

Briefly, gluttony has to do with our overindulgence with food. Lust, unlike love, is to make use of a person's body for sexual gratification. Greed is the hoarding of material goods to secure the future. Sadness is a form of self-pity due to comparing ourselves with others who are better off than us. Anger is caused by hurt or injury that we receive from others. Apathy or sloth hits us when we lack the passion or desire for spiritual matters. Vainglory is when we think we are better than others and want people to take note of our spiritual progress. Pride is when the self takes over the place of God and not giving him the credit for our spiritual advancement.[7]

Thirst for God

The most important function of the roots is, of course, to provide nutrients and water for the tree to survive. The roots are the beginning of the vascular system that moves water. The vascular system has two parts: the *xylem* transports water and minerals from the roots to the crown of the tree while the *phloem* conducts, in the opposite direction, by transporting the sugars produced by photosynthesis from the leaves down the trunk to the roots. Like the plants in our garden that change their direction towards light, the roots also grow in the direction of the nutrients like nitrates,

---

7. For a more detailed description of the list, see Mah, *Garden of the Soul,* 22–24.

potassium, or phosphates. They can locate these nutrients even in minute quantities. The roots' "thirst" for water is important for tree growth. A typical tree consumes a huge amount of water. Ninety percent of the water will be lost into the atmosphere through transpiration and only ten percent is used up for plant growth. Good roots will sink deep into the soil in search for water. Likewise, Christians must develop a thirst for God in their hearts in order to be firmly rooted in Jesus. This "thirst" that God creates in us is a call to follow him. We are seeking God because deep down in the core of our souls we feel that we are being sought by him. Thomas Kelly writes:

> A deep-throated bell, muffled or clear, comes ringing in the ears of our souls from a distant shore in Eternity and awakens in us a vague uneasiness, a homesickness, a longing. We've all heard that bell, distant or clear, calling us to a vaster life. Like a wild duck who has paused to pick at the straws of a barnyard, but who finds a dim stirring, a homing instinct which makes him leave the sticks and straws and easy comfortable food for the body and wing his way into the blue south sky, where lies his home, so do you and I have a voice within us, a homing instinct of the soul which whispers within us uneasiness and urgency, and the call of Eternity for our souls. We are all seekers, for we feel we are sought.[8]

Hole in the Heart

When God created us he made a void in our hearts that only he could satisfy. This God-shaped vacuum, at the core of our human identity, creates a thirst or longing for God. Only God can fill this hole for us. This desire, at the core of our souls, is crowded out by other desires that beg for our attention. This deep longing implanted by God causes us to be restless. In our restlessness, we look out for other things in life in order to plug the hole in our hearts. We look for fulfillment in material things, in entertainment, in leisure, in our hobbies, in jobs, in relationships, and many more. We

8. Cited by Whitmire, *Plain Living*, 102.

are thus on a false quest to pursue these things while avoiding our need for God to quench our thirst. While looking for many ways to quench our thirst, we find ourselves far from our true home. C. S. Lewis recognized that "the deepest thirst within us is not adapted to the deepest nature of the world" was because as mortals we were far from our true home.⁹ He further reasoned that if he found in himself "a desire which no experience in this world can satisfy, the most probable explanation is that I was made for another world."¹⁰

If we know that we do not belong here then we are ready to make our way to our true home. The psalmist, who lost all that he had and exiled to a strange land, longed to return home. He cried out in song: "As a deer pants for streams of water, so my soul pants for you, O God. My soul thirsts for God, for the living God. When can I go and meet with God?" (Ps 42:1–2). This journey home usually runs through a desert place. Our thirst for God is even made more acute when we face a desert-like experience in our lives. The psalmist cries out saying, "My soul thirsts for you, my body longs for you, in a dry and weary land where there is no water" (Ps 63:1). The soul that seeks after God will almost always face some desert-like experiences in his life. David Benner's *Spirituality and the Awakening Self* highlights some desert-like experiences that can propel us to take the journey home.¹¹ These experiences can come from the circumstances of life: a nasty divorce, financial failure, vocational disillusionment, sickness, loss due to death or accidents. We hear testimonies of Christians who, after a period of difficulty and severe struggle, begin to take their faith and walk with God more seriously. Psychological symptoms like depression, anxiety, uncontrolled anger, and irritation can also be potential awakenings.¹²

---

9. Lewis, *Pilgrim's Regress*, 148.

10. Lewis, *Mere Christianity*, 106.

11. Benner, *Spirituality and the Awakening Self*, 7–9.

12. The material in this section is taken from Mah, *Take Up Your Mat and Walk*, 19. For a more detailed discussion of the "deserts" in our life, please read Mah, *Garden of the Soul*, 81–83.

Give Time to God

We must give time and space for God to work in our lives if we want to take charge of our inner life and be firmly rooted in Jesus. Busyness and hurry do violence to the health and growth of the soul. As Ann Voskamp, noted author of *One Thousand Gifts*, puts it, "Hurry always empties a soul."[13] A life packed with activities has no space and time for God. Roots do not grow well in compacted soil. A few days ago I was preparing a pot of soil to grow some blue pea flowers. I used an old flower pot which previously housed a palm plant that had withered and died. I carefully removed the dead roots, digging and turning the soil to get rid of all the root remnants, stones, and weeds from the pot. I planted some seeds in the soil and hopefully, with enough water and light, it would slowly sprout and grow.

For some time, city engineers were puzzled why trees grew into pipes in the first place.[14] The initial understanding was that the roots were attracted to the moisture around the pipes. Later, they discovered that it was not the case. The roots were attracted to the loose soil around the pipe's vicinity. The soil was not compacted after the construction of the pipes. The loose soil allowed the roots to breathe. Trees have to work harder against the concrete hard ground to get to the loose soil in an urban setting. Some of the roots penetrated the seal between sections of the pipe and grew inside them. The trenches built to lay pipes provided such a "breathing" space for trees to extend their roots in search of water and minerals.

Unless we give time to nurture our inner life, we will not progress in our spiritual lives. Activities, even Christian ones, can become a hindrance if these take away our time from paying attention to God. We all know very well the story of Martha and Mary. While Martha was attending to Jesus' every need, Mary was paying attention to Jesus' every word. We expect Mary to help out and chide her for not extending a helping hand to relieve Martha. To

---

13. Voskamp, *One Thousand Gifts*, 67.
14. Wohlleben, *The Hidden Life of Trees*, 175–76.

our surprise, the story took an unexpected twist. Mary was the one commended by Jesus instead of Martha! We feel awkward about this story because deep inside us, we behave more like Martha than Mary. I was disturbed when one of my professors wrote that busyness was essentially laziness. Eugene Peterson, in *Subversive Spirituality*, writes:

> Busyness is the enemy of spirituality. It is essentially laziness. It is doing the easy thing instead of the hard thing. It is filing our time with our own actions instead of paying attention to God's actions. It is taking charge.[15]

Instead of letting God take over by receiving orders from him, busyness can be a way for us to avoid that by taking control of our lives. Jesus made sure that he spent time alone with God even though he was busy. He could only do what the Father wanted him to do because he wanted God to take charge of his life (John 5:19). We must first be a Mary before we can be an effective Martha. We must pay attention to God before we can attend to him.

The Kingdom of God

What does it mean to be rooted in Jesus? It means to follow Jesus in his teachings and way of life. The teachings of Jesus revolve around the Kingdom of God. What is the Kingdom of God? What does it involve? It involves "the range of God's effective will, where what God wants done is done."[16] Right now the effective will of God is not completely fulfilled on earth though it is present and available to all who seek after it. God's reign, like the mustard seed, will grow to its complete fulfillment at a future date that only God knows. Meanwhile, it is our prayer that God's kingdom will come and his will be done on earth as it is in heaven. Practically, it means to carry this vision of participating "by our actions in what God is doing now in our lifetime on earth."[17] To obey and follow the

---

15. Peterson, *Subversive Spirituality*, Page not found.
16. Willard, *Renewing the Mind of Christ*, 17.
17. Willard, *Renewing the Mind of Christ*, 17.

example of Jesus in his teachings and way of life are to live and participate in God's kingdom.

The keyword used to describe the Kingdom of God is "deliverance".[18] Jesus, the anointed one, was sent to proclaim good news to the poor, to bind the brokenhearted, to proclaim freedom to the captives, and release from darkness for the prisoners (Isa 61:1). God's kingdom is his reign over us when he delivers us from the bondage of sin. Deliverance of lost souls from sin and eternal condemnation is a prime work of God's kingdom. Yet, there are many sectors in our world today that need to be delivered from the bondage of sin. In kingdom work, we should also pay attention to works that include peacemaking, overcoming injustice and violence, helping the poor and oppressed, and healing the blind and sick.

A disciplined life is necessary to carry out this vision of God's kingdom and to make it a reality. We need to be spiritually formed in our inner life before our outer life can correspond to the ethos of God's kingdom. Dallas Willard, Christian philosopher and intellectual, has this to say:

> We come to grips with who we really are, inside and out. For we will do what we are. So we will need to become the kind of person who routinely and easily walk in the goodness and power of Jesus our master . . . In the degree to which such a spiritual transformation to inner Christlikeness is successful, the outer life of the individual will become a natural expression or outflow of the character and teachings of Jesus.[19]

Solitude and Silence

The way to open our lives for God to do his work in the inner self is through the practice of spiritual disciplines.[20] Spiritual disciplines are the means for God's grace to work in our inner being. Spiritual

---

18. Stassen, "Kingdom of God" 561–62.
19. Willard, *Renewing the Mind of Christ*, 12.
20. Willard, *Renewing the Mind of Christ*, 31.

disciplines, by themselves, are not able to do much. They will not benefit us spiritually if we do the disciplines for the sake of doing them. Spiritual disciplines, if used correctly and with good intentions, help us to focus on God, get close to God, be open to receive his love, and be responsive to his leading in our lives. God, through the spiritual disciplines, will shape and remake our personalities that follow and pattern after the life of Jesus. Only then are we able to fulfill our calling (Eph 4:1).

Like Willard, I want to highlight solitude and silence as a discipline that is much needed for modern day Christians.[21] Solitude and silence will shield us from the "noise" that we receive from the world at all times. We are assaulted with all kinds of visual, aural, and physical stimuli that compete for our attention. They entice us with words like "taste me, use me, love me, follow me, and buy me." The world consistently calls on us to yield ourselves to its seductive ways. It caters to our instinctive need for security, control, and affection. It prevents us from getting in touch with the true self which resides at the core of our souls. Like the prodigal son, the lure of worldly pleasures that cater to our fleshly desires prevents us from getting in touch with our desire for God. Our lives become fragmented and lacking focus. The need for solitude and silence, in a world of consumerism and compulsive behavior, is clearly explained by Thomas Merton.

> For as long as we live in our exterior consciousness alone, and identify ourselves completely with the superficial and transient side of our existence, then we are completely immersed in an unreality. And to cling with passion to a state of unreality is the root of all sin: technically known as pride. It is the affirmation of our non-being as the ultimate reality for which we live, as against the being and truth of God. Hence we must become detached from the unreality that is in us in order to be united to the reality that lies deeper within and is our true self - our inmost self-in-God.[22]

21. For practical help in the discipline of solitude and silence, please read *Take Up Your Mat and Walk*, 98–101.

22. Merton, "The Inner Experience: Infused Contemplation (V)" 76.

We need to develop our inner life if we want to live the Christian life according to the ethos of God's kingdom. Like the roots of the tree, this inner work of our souls takes time and much patience to develop. Our spiritual health and vitality depend on it. It is also an area of our Christian life that we tend to neglect simply because it is not visible to the outside world and is not achievement orientated. Besides, it takes a lot of discipline for us to nurture its growth. Results do not come readily and we need to wait patiently for it to bear fruit. On the other hand, it is much easier for us to live our Christian lives outwardly by engaging in various activities, religious or otherwise. Our busyness, whether in church, at home or the marketplace may be a subtle way of not willing to let go and let God take over our lives. It is a form of control over our time and resources.

To be rooted in Jesus, we need to acquire a thirst for God. Often this thirst gets stronger when we undergo a desert-like experience in our lives. God will use these encounters to force us to pay closer attention to our inner selves. When things around us are getting out of control, we will look inward for strength and stability in order to overcome the storms lashing at our lives. Solitude and silence is a good discipline that helps us develop the inner life. It helps to still our soul before him. When we enter into a period of solitude and silence we enter into the wilderness of our souls when we begin to pay close attention to God's miraculous work in our lives. Shielded from the noise in the world and our own inner noise, we begin to be still and know that he is God (Ps 46:10). Sue Monk Kidd shared how she could be still before God:

> I often found a still point by lighting a candle and watching its silent flame for five or ten minutes, my heart warm and focused on God. Sometimes I paused to reflect on the pictures and symbols in my study . . . Other times I returned to the still point by taking a few silent minutes to stroll under the stars in the backyard, listen to music,

or curl up with my sketch pad. The idea is to still ourselves, to draw ourselves back to the deeper life that flows beneath the surface of our days.[23]

---

23. Kidd, *When the Heart Waits*, 126.

3

The Communal Life

The community of the saints is not an 'ideal'
community consisting of perfect and sinless
men and women, where there is no need of further repentance.
No, it is a community which proves that it is
worthy of the gospel of forgiveness
by constantly and sincerely proclaiming God's forgiveness.
—Dietrich Bonhoeffer

Trees are Social Beings

Most of us do not know that trees are social beings. Trees stand alone by themselves and we hardly see any social connections between them. The social activities happen below ground. They are connected to each other through a massive social network formed by the root systems that are hidden from sight. There are of course advantages for trees to work together in communities. A single tree cannot do much but a forest of trees can influence the local climate. The forest, besides storing water and generating humidity, also moderates the temperature from extreme heat and cold. Those who enter a forest will know that the climatic environment inside the forest is different from the outside. The air is fresh and cool in the forest. Every single tree in the community is important because any gaps in the forest will have adverse effects. Strong winds enter these openings to uproot the trees and dry up the forest floor causing the moisture to evaporate into the air.[1] The back of my house faces a small hill. Lately, a strong gale hit the area where I live. The storm uprooted several trees. I noticed that the uprooted trees were located in the area of the forest where they were most exposed to the elements.

It is interesting to note that trees can recognize one another. A study, done by Massimo Maffei from Turin University, shows that plants and trees can distinguish their own roots from those of their own kind and other species.[2] If we look up at the forest canopy we discover a phenomenon called "crown shyness". This happens mostly to trees of the same species. They tend not to intrude into the space of nearby trees. Crown shyness is a phenomenon where trees avoid touching one another at the upper branches of the forest canopy. If we look up we can see clearly marked borders of cracks or lines on the canopy of the forest. Trees seem to know and recognize their own kind. Likewise, Christians recognize one another as part of the community of faith.

The Need for Community

The people of God are called the "ekklesia" which means "the called out" ones. They are called to leave their old ways of life and to begin a new life under God. Christians cannot live in isolation. The moment they become a child of God they belong to the community of God's people. In fact, the existence of the Christian community is based on the divine call of God.[3] It is not based on any human initiative due to social ties, economic advantages, mu-

---

1. Wohlleben, *The Hidden Life of Trees*, 3–4.
2. Wohlleben, *The Hidden Life of Trees*, 3.
3. Nouwen, *Reaching Out*, 153.

tual benefits or shared goals. Most human communities exist for the common good of the members. Christian communities are different. Members of the community do not exist for themselves but for God. The community exists for God's kingdom and can only be sustained by him alone. He is the source of the community's life and existence. It is through Christ and in Christ that Christians exist as a community of believers.[4] A community of God's people is needed to help the Christian fulfill his or her call. The encouragement and strength of liked minded believers will help the believer to keep alive the call of God.

The first thing that Jesus did was to create a community when he was called by God the Father to go on a mission. He called his first disciples. He built up this small community from scratch. He showed the disciples, by word and life, what it meant to live in God's kingdom. He was patient with them. Communities cannot be built overnight. It takes time for people to feel a sense of belonging and to live together. Jesus called on the community to support him at the most critical juncture of his mission. He called on his disciples at Gethsemane to pray with him as he underwent the greatest struggle of his entire mission. Even after the resurrection, Jesus' first contact was to appear before his people. Paul not only prayed earnestly for the Thessalonian Christians but also wished to see them in order to encourage them in the faith (1 Thess 3:10). The apostle John would rather see his own people face to face than writing to them. "I have much to write to you, but I do not want to use paper and ink. Instead, I hope to visit you and talk to you face to face, so that our joy may be complete" (2 John 12).

Loving God and Neighbor

Jesus once told his disciples that he would be with them when two or three were gathered together in his name (Matt 18:20). This, according to the usual interpretation, refers to the church. The church is where God's people come together (even if there are

---

4. Bonhoeffer, *Life Together*, 10.

only two persons) to invoke God's name in prayers and worship. There is also another interpretation that is not commonly known. The "two" does not refer to people but to the two laws of God. It refers to the two commands of God: to love him and to love one's neighbor. This interpretation was given to Catherine of Siena.[5] The activities of a genuine community must reflect these two commands. Prayer plays a central role in community life because it is the greatest expression of our love for God.[6] Prayer cannot exist only at the personal and individual level. It has to be shared. If prayer is expressing our love for God then this love can only be reflected in the way we treat other members of the community. It is not possible to love God without involving our neighbors in the community. We cannot love God without also loving our neighbors and pray on their behalf. Our prayers go beyond our private needs to the needs of the larger community. Community will deepen and broaden our prayers because it keeps us from only focusing on ourselves and our private needs. We need the support of the community to grow our prayer life.[7]

Prayer and service go hand in hand with a community. Our expression of God's love in words must also be translated into action by serving one another. Paul's image of a human body to describe the Christian community is most imaginative and challenging. No member of the body is indispensable and adequate in itself. It needs the support of others for it to reach its full potential. We can do greater and better things with others in the community than doing by ourselves alone. As Joan Chittister, a former prioress of the Benedictine Order, comments: "Alone, I am what I am, but in community, I have the chance to become everything that I can be."[8] Love can be costly and demanding. We know that it is not easy to serve. It takes humility, patience, and sacrifice to minister to others. Life together in the community is not for our own convenience. It is for Christ's sake and "is a sign of the power of

5. Maricle, *Deeply Rooted*, 58.
6. Nouwen, *Reaching Out*, 152.
7. Nouwen, *Reaching Out*, 151–52.
8. Chittister, *Wisdom Distilled from the Daily*, 49.

Christian community to others."[9] The world, according to Jesus, will know that we are his disciples when we love one another. We are to shine our light before the world so that when they see our good deeds they will praise our God in heaven (Matt 5:16).

No Perfect Community

No community is perfect. Many avoid the Christian community because of the difficult people in the church. I am sure many of us do have a fair share of dealing with people who are unreasonable, lacking kindness, offensive, and not loving. Conflicts among the brothers and sisters are common in the churches (Phil 4:2). Relationships get soured and difficult to resolve. Some ongoing conflicts have been simmering under the surface for quite a while and conflicting parties talk past one another.

Others avoid the church because there are too many rules to follow and pitfalls to avoid. The church takes on a Pharisaical mode of existence. There are little space and freedom for members to express themselves for fear of flouting one of these rules. Members' loyalty is questioned when these rules or religious protocol are not followed closely.

There are others who find the church too impersonal and utilitarian. People are valued and treated based not on relationships but on functions - how well they can contribute to the community life. Goals are set and programs are planned to achieve these goals. The church community is defined, critiqued, and evaluated based on the success of these goals. The church has lost its community spirit. The less functional members of the Body of Christ are left out and are treated as impediments to the church life. The more valuable members of the church are highly valued and sought after. The church, that exists purely along functional rather than communal lines, will cease to be a community.

Others have difficulty belonging to the church because the language used is too elitist and not down to earth. The language

---

9. Chittister, *Wisdom Distilled from the Daily*, 45.

has too many theological buzzwords. Some words that preachers use on the pulpit need careful exegetical analysis before they make sense to the uninformed. They sound too "theological" and "heavy" for the untrained ear to follow through. There is too much ambiguity in the use of words. They often sound hollow and thin. The language used must promote a sense of belonging rather than estrangement. The words, spoken or otherwise, must come from the heart and not from the mind only. Kathleen Norris, award-winning poet and author, shares her experience:

> When I first ventured back to Sunday worship in my small town, the service felt like a word bombardment, an hour-long barrage of heavyweight theological terminology. Often, I was so exhausted afterwards that I would spend a three-hour nap. And I would wake up depressed, convinced that this world called "Christian" was closed to me.[10]

The Christian Community

There is no perfect community. We should not aim to be one. God is using our flaws to teach us patience and perseverance that are essential for the formation of our souls. A true community should not aim for perfection but growth. People join communities in order for their needs to be met. Communities provide a sense of belonging and members find meaning in being together. Communal groups focus on providing the needs of their members. The Christian community is different. It is a "waiting" community in anticipation of what God can do for its members. The church is on a pilgrimage. It is always moving forward in anticipation of what is to come.[11] The church is not a shelter or oasis where members feel comfortable meeting the needs of one another. Henri Nouwen encourages members of the community to say to each other, "We are together, but we cannot fulfill each other . . . we help each other,

---

10. Norris, *Amazing Grace*, 7.
11. Nouwen, *Reaching Out*, 153,155.

but we also have to remind each other that our destiny is beyond our togetherness."[12]

There is no ideal Christian community. Bonhoeffer, the German theologian, warns against Christians who seem to have a definite vision on how a Christian community should behave and look like. They will easily get disillusioned when their expectations are not met. This is a wish dream that will never happen. God, in his grace and mercy, will shatter such dreams. The shock of disillusionment may be a good thing for members of the Christian community. Only then will they begin to take hold of the promise by faith which God has already prepared for her. Church members can experience genuine fellowship if they overcome this crisis and abandon their illusive ideals. Instead of making demands on themselves, on others, and on God, they should be thankful that God has made them a part of the community. God has already laid the only foundation of their fellowship by binding them into one body with other believers in Jesus Christ long before they enter into the life of the community.[13] Bonhoeffer has this to say:

> Innumerable times a whole Christian community has broken down because it sprung from a wish dream. The serious Christian, set down for the first time in a Christian community, is likely to bring with him a very definite idea of what Christian life together should be like and try to realize it. But God's grace speedily shatters such dreams. Just as God desires to lead us to a knowledge of genuine Christian fellowship, so surely must we be overwhelmed by a great disillusionment with others, with Christians in general, and if we are fortunate, with ourselves . . . Every human dream that is injected into the Christian community is a hindrance to genuine community and must be banished if genuine community is to survive.[14]

---

12. Nouwen, *Reaching out*, 153.
13. Bonhoeffer, *Life Together*, 15–16.
14. Bonhoeffer, *Life Together*, 15.

The Importance of Community

Why does living in a genuine community important to the Christian? We know the reasons why some people avoid the Christian community. Peterson, the author of *The Message,* confessed at times that he preferred the company of those outside his congregation who were not following Jesus. But he knew deep down that this preference could not be justified according to Scripture. He wrote:

> I didn't come to the conviction easily, but finally there was no getting around it: there can be no maturity in the spiritual life, no obedience in following Jesus, no wholeness in the Christian life apart from an immersion and embrace of community.[15]

The question, for Peterson and for believers everywhere, is not whether they should belong to the community of faith but how are they going to live as active members within this community. Knowing the reasons why community living is good for the believer is helpful in this regard.

A Place to Serve

First, the community provides an avenue for members to serve one another. It provides the space where talents and gifts are used to meet the needs of the Body of Christ. In Psalm 133 we read that the unity of God's people, which is good and pleasant, is like the oil that is "poured on the head, running down on the beard, running down on Aaron's beard, down upon the collar of his robes." Oil was used in the ordination of Aaron and priests (Exod 29:7,9). The anointing was to set them apart for works of service. Christians, who are chosen and belonged to God, are priests in the holy nation (1 Pet 2:9). They play a priestly role, set apart by the anointing of the Holy Spirit, to minister to one another. Paul wrote to the Corinthian church saying that the different kinds of gifts, service, and

---

15. Peterson, *Christ Plays in Ten Thousand Places,* 226.

workings came from the same Spirit and "he gave them to each one... for the common good (1 Cor 12: 4–7,11). Church members who understand the body life of Christ will use their gifts not to compete but to complement each other for the sake of the love and unity they have in Christ.

A Place to Reveal God

Second, coming together has its advantages. We are able to see the work of God manifested in the lives of believers. We often think we are the only ones struggling with our faith. We falsely believe that we have problems that are unique to our situation. We envy others for their strong faith. When people with diverse experiences and challenges share their lives in the community we begin to notice the workings of God among his people. God is not "hidden" or out of reach. He is actively at work in the lives of his children. Our faith is renewed, strengthened, and rejuvenated when we hear testimonies of fellow believers talking about their struggles and faith in God. It is like the "dew of Hermon falling on Mount Zion" (Ps 133:3). The drier parts around Jerusalem will surely welcome the cool moisture that flows down from the highest mountain in Israel. We draw solace and strength from the community when our faith is weak and our spiritual lives become dry. The changed lives in our midst amaze and surprise us. With eager expectation we look forward to what God is doing in the lives of the believers in our fellowship. Peterson comments:

> A community of faith flourishes when we view each other with this expectancy, wondering what God will do today in this one, in that one. When we are in a community with those Christ loves and redeems, we are constantly finding out new things about them.[16]

---

16. Peterson, *A Long Obedience in the Same Direction*, 182.

A Place to Witness

Third, the community also projects the face of God to the world.[17] As God's people, we bear witness to God's presence and power to the world. How else does the world know our God? It is through his people that the world knows who God is. Jesus says that the world will know that we are his disciples when we love one another. The early Christians were known for their love and hospitality. The love of the Christians even took the Roman emperor Julian by surprise. Julian, who was anti-Christian, made this observation:

> Atheism has been specially advanced through the loving service rendered to strangers, and through their care for the burial of the dead. It is a scandal that there is not a single Jew who is a beggar, and that the godless Galileans care not only for their own poor but ours as well; while those who belong to us look in vain for the help that we should render them.[18]

According to Tertullian, the father of Latin Christianity, even pagans confessed that the Christians truly loved one another. The charitable projects cared by Christians included burying the poor, supplying the needs of boys and girls who were deprived, helping the elderly who were too weak to leave their homes, providing for those who suffered shipwreck, and gave to those who were banished to hard labor in mines and islands for their faith in Christ.[19]

A Place for Each Other

Fourth, the community creates a conducive atmosphere for members to worship, pray, and celebrate together. Of course, we can worship, pray, and celebrate alone by ourselves. But it is different when these are done in a group. A shared joy is a double joy. That's the reason why we want to celebrate our birthdays and

---

17. LaNoue, *The Spiritual Legacy of Henri Nouwen*, 119.

18. Cited by Neill, *A History of Christian Missions*, 42. Emperor Julian called Christians "atheists" because they did not worship the Roman gods.

19. Foster, *Freedom of Simplicity*, 62–63.

anniversaries with others and not just by ourselves alone. The Bible says that we are to run the race surrounded by a great cloud of witnesses (Heb 12:1). God does not intend for us to run alone. Throughout the New Testament, God calls on us to do things to one another. The words "one another" and "each other" are used many times and in many places in the New Testament exhorting Christians not to neglect the life together in the community.

Paul uses the image of the physical body metaphorically to illustrate the importance of participating in the life of the community. The body can express itself well when all its members are working together. The legs can run or jump well but the body will not go far if the rest of the members are not involved. The arms provide balance to the body. How about tying our arms around the body and try running or jumping and see what will happen to us? The eyes and ears will prevent the body from knocking into obstacles while it is moving. How about blindfolding our eyes and try running or jumping around? Paul says that each member of Christ's body belongs to all the others. He does not say that each member belongs only to its own (Rom 12:5). We stand a better chance of doing something greater and better when we are a part of the community than just being alone. The sum is always greater than its parts.

A True Community

To be human is to know who we are. We cannot discover who we are by ourselves. We know who we are through others. The human need to belong is a universal need. Our identities are forged through belonging to a group where we learn from each other and depend on each other. Belonging also gives us a sense of security and self-worth. To belong is to open up to others. This is where we grow and mature in mutual dependency. However, a group can close-in on itself if it is not careful. The very strength of any group can become its weakness. The identity and security that a group provides can lead the group to be exclusive. The group excludes others out of fear. The heart of prejudice and exclusion, according to Jean Vanier, is fear. On the other hand, trust is at the root of all forms of inclusion.[20] Fear will prevent the group from changing and moving forward. A closed group that feels superior will resist any changes to its existing order. The group will resist strongly any differences in order to maintain the culture of liked-mindedness by sharing the same goals and interests. Living and doing things together may not necessarily make a community.

A true community has its center in Christ. Members who are bonded in Christ to this Center share a common vision of God. In this way, friendships are realigned and differences are leveled. Old friendships are discarded and new ones are established. Social, cultural, and educational differences no longer become barriers. People who show potential tend to disappoint and those whom we dismiss earlier show great prospects and enthusiasm for God. These are the ones who live lives at the Center. They make us feel welcome into the fellowship. They accept us as we are. Trust is carefully nurtured in the soil of unconditional love. Within this circle of trust, our souls feel safe and are given the opportunity to emerge and grow. Palmer, when talking about the circle of trust, has this to say:

> The people who help us grow toward true self offer unconditional love, neither judging us to be deficient nor trying to force us to change but accepting us exactly as we are . . . Here is one way to understand the relationships in the circle of trust: they combine unconditional love, or regard, with hopeful expectancy, creating a space that both safeguards and encourages the inner journey.[21]

Steps Toward a True Community

Several precautions need to be taken in order to maintain a true community. These steps taken may not be exhaustive. I will highlight here what I feel are needed in all communities of God. First, diversities and differences within the group must be condoned and

---

20. Vanier, *Becoming Human*, 71, 73.
21. Palmer, *A Hidden Wholeness*, 60.

not condemned. In fact, it should be celebrated. This is in line with Paul's use of the body metaphor to describe the Church. Differences will challenge the group from being clannish and excluding others. The exercise of unconditional love and a common vision of God will help transcend the many individual differences within the group.

Second, the group should be wary of an ideological mindset that says "this is the way things are done here" and is not used to new ways of doing things. The group is no longer moving forward when members become comfortable with the status quo. On the other hand, new patterns or group dynamics should be considered carefully when introduced into the life of the Christian community.[22] Whatever is introduced must not undermine our understanding as a community set apart and called by God. The values and behaviors that under-gird the community should not be compromised.

Third, the language we use in the community is important. The language must reflect our dependence on God who is the one who calls us to live life together. Whatever activities or programs we have as a group must be shaped, formed, and informed by prayer. Prayer puts Christ as the center of the group's existence. Nouwen believes that prayer is the language of the community and it is through prayer that the community is created as well as expressed. Without prayer, "the community quickly degenerates into a club with a common cause but no common vocation."[23]

Fourth, we need to develop trust among members of the community. The lack of trust will lead to all kinds of fears that will break down the life of the community. Fears give rise to conflicts that sour relationships among members. When we lack trust we will not be opened to each other. We become possessive, overbearing, and lacking the freedom and openness to grow into spiritual maturity. We are judgmental and critical of things and people in the community. This problem afflicts many churches and is the

---

22. Nouwen, *Reaching Out*, 155.
23. Nouwen, *Reaching Out*, 156.

main reason why churches cannot grow and become effective witnesses to the world.

When Jesus calls us to follow him, he also calls us to live a communal life. We learn from trees the need and importance of community living. The Christian community is different from other types of communities that we are familiar with. The Christian community exists not for ourselves but for God and his kingdom. It is within a communal setting that the love for God and for neighbor is fully expressed. It is manifested through our prayers to God and service for others. Prayer and service are the two pillars of a Christian community. Perhaps this is the reason why we call our Sunday gathering a "worship service". Community living provides the Christian an opportunity to worship God and serve one another.

God reveals himself more fully when saints live life together in a communal setting. At the same time, the world gets to know God through the love of saints expressed in community living. Community living will help the child of God to live out his or her calling more effectively. It is easy for any group to become exclusive and the tendency to take strong measures to maintain the status quo. Steps need to be taken intentionally to prevent this from happening. A true community celebrates diversity and differences within the group. It is forward-looking and is open to new ways of doing things. The community's life is centered in Christ as its Head and is shaped, formed, and informed by prayer. Building trust among members is key to the health and vitality of the group's life.

4

The Sacrificial Life

If anyone would come after me, he must deny himself
and take up his cross and follow me.
For whoever wants to save his life will lose it,
but whoever loses his life for me and for the gospel will save it

—Mark 8:34–35

Two Stories of Sacrifice

SHEL SILVERSTEIN'S CLASSIC TALE of *The Giving Tree* has touched the hearts of many people. People are drawn to the story because they can easily identify with the tree's sacrificial giving. The story is about a tree's love for a boy. The boy played with the tree when he was a young kid. He would climb up her trunk, swing from her branches, and eat her apples. He would sleep under her shade when he was tired. The tree was happy because the boy loved playing with her. When he got older things changed. He was no longer playing like before. He asked the tree whether he could have her apples because he wanted to earn some money. The tree obliged. Then he came back again and this time asked if he could build a house for his family. The tree obliged. The tree gave him her branches to build a house. After a long while, the boy who had grown much older came and asked for her trunk to build a boat. Again the tree was happy to oblige. The boy was old and worn out when he met the tree for the last time. The boy told the tree that he had nothing much to ask from her for he was tired and he just needed a place to sit and rest. The tree was reduced to a stump at this time. She straightened herself up as much as she could in order for the boy to sit down and rest on an old stump. Again she was happy to oblige.

As a young Christian, I was touched by another story of sacrifice. John and Betty Stam were young missionaries to China. They worked with the China Inland Mission in the 1930s. They were married in China and had a daughter named Helen Priscilla. One day without warning, the town where they served was attacked by the Communists. They were captured and ransom money was asked for their release. They were forced to march through the streets and were finally beheaded. Fortunately, Helen was smuggled out by some courageous Chinese Christians. John's letter was found hidden inside the clothing and blanket of little Helen days before the massacre. John wrote:

> Dear Brethren, My wife, baby and myself are today in the hands of the Communists in the city of Tsingteh. Their demand is twenty thousand dollars for our release. All our possessions and stores are in their hands, but we praise God for peace in our hearts and a meal tonight. God grant you wisdom in what you do, and us fortitude, courage and peace of heart. He is able and a wonderful Friend in such a time. Things happened so quickly this a.m. They were in the city just a few hours after the ever-persistent rumors really became alarming, so that we could not prepare to leave in time. We were just too late. The Lord bless and guide you, and as for us, may God be glorified whether by life or by death.[1]

---

1. Carl Stam, "John and Betty Stam"

Inspired by the Cross

Tertullian, the Church Father, once said that the blood of the martyrs was seed. Indeed the testimony of John and Betty Stam in China caused many to take heed to the missionary call overseas. We always think that only missionaries can make sacrifices for God. This is not true. It is expected of all Christians to heed the call to sacrifice for God. This is the appeal of Paul to the Roman Christians.

> Therefore I urge you, brothers, in view of God's mercy, to offer your bodies as living sacrifices, holy and pleasing to God—this is your spiritual act of worship (Rom 12:1).

Whatever sacrifices we make for God are inspired by the Cross of Christ. When Paul wrote to the Corinthian Church concerning the subject of giving, he put the sincerity of their love to the test by making two comparisons. He mentioned the generosity of the Macedonian churches and, at the same time, pointed to Christ who "though he was rich, yet for your sake he became poor, so that you through his poverty might become rich" (2 Cor 8:9). They became "rich" through the generosity of Jesus who had given his life for them at the cross. The Corinthian Christians knew about this because they had experienced this grace of Jesus in their lives. When Paul writes that we should offer ourselves as living sacrifices in view of God's mercy, he is referring to what he has written in the previous chapters of Romans (1–11). This is the reason he uses the word "therefore" at the beginning of the verse. In these chapters, Paul says that God has been merciful to us because through the death and resurrection of Jesus Christ we are no longer condemned by sin. We are justified by faith and reconciled to God with an everlasting hope. We are now called to live a life worthy of his Name based on God's mercies. We do that by offering our bodies as living sacrifices to him.

Surrendering Our Bodies

Sacrifices were offered as part of worship to God in the Old Testament. The concept of sacrifice used by Paul in the New Testament is not a sin offering like in the Old Testament. It is rather an offering signifying our thankfulness for the forgiveness we receive at the cross. It is an offering of dedicating or consecrating our lives to God. It has to do with the way we live in this sinful world. We should conduct ourselves, using our bodies to glorify God by offering them as instruments of righteousness (Rom 6:13). Our bodies do not belong to us anymore for we are bought with a price. Therefore we are to honor God with our bodies (1 Cor 6:19–20). We are not like the world for we are holy as God is holy. Our conduct and lifestyle in the world must seek God's pleasure and not to please ourselves and the people around us. Only then can we truly worship God by bringing worth and praise to him. Worship is not confined only to a specific place or time like on Sundays. Worship embraces all aspects of our lives at all times. Bill Tisdale, a missionary to the Philippines, describes surrendering the different parts of his body in a prayer to Christ.

> Lord, here are my eyes. I give them to you. I want them to see only the things you want them to see. Help me to always look at the things you want to look at and avoid the things you do not want to look at. Here are my hands. Work through my hands to do what you want to do. Here are my feet. Guide them to go where you want them to go. I give you the lordship of my body.[2]

No Conformity to the World

Paul calls on Christians not to conform to the pattern of the world but be transformed by the renewing of the mind (Rom 12:2). We can only offer our bodies as instruments of righteousness if we are counter-cultural Christians. The prevailing culture will challenge and weaken our faith if our minds are contaminated by its godless

---

2. Cited by Willis, Jr. *Master Life*, 97.

The Sacrificial Life

concepts and practices. The Bible calls on God's people to be different from others. Israel must not adopt the practices of the Egyptians and the Canaanites (Lev 18:3–4). She must not conform to the standards of the nations around her (Ezek 11:12). Jesus called on his followers not to follow the practices of the pagans (Matt 6:8). His lack of compromise with the religious establishment led to his death at the Cross.

The Early Christians faced persecution because they refused to conform to the prevailing practices of the Greco-Roman world.[3] Religious syncretism and emperor worship were stumbling blocks for the Christians. Imperial policy took on these two practices in order to foster political unity within the empire. With the expansion of the empire, more foreign gods from other lands were added to the Roman Pantheon, a temple that housed numerous gods. To Rome's vested interested, all gods whatever their names were the same gods. This posed a problem to Christians who believed in the uniqueness of Christ and the worship of the one true God. The same prohibition applied to emperor worship. Refusing to burn incense before the emperor was a sign of treason and disloyalty.

Today's Christians may face a different set of problems or trends in the prevailing culture.[4] Pluralism, like in the days of the Roman empire, still exists today. All religions, in whatever stripes and shapes, are valid and should be not be condemned but tolerated and respected. This may prove to be a challenge to many Christians in Asia where the family altar houses a variety of gods. Christianity's claim to be the only true way is offensive to many people. Christians are deemed to be intolerant and arrogant people. Moral laxity, like in Paul's time, has been a challenge for many Christians today. The situation is made worse because of the easy access to new social media technologies that allow users to have access to all kinds of information anonymously. Christians are exposed to all kinds of immoralities that cater to the lustful flesh. The consumer culture, making use of clever advertisements

---

3. Gonzalez, *The Story of Christianity,* 14–16.

4. Stott points out four trends: pluralism, materialism, ethical relativism, and narcissism. *The Radical Disciple,* 21–26.

and peer pressure, entices many Christians to live a materialistic lifestyle that is beyond their means. Many are in debt because of this. Upgrading one's lifestyle and money making occupy most of their time. This will affect their walk with God and their witness in the world.

Paying the Price

Non-conformity to the ways of the world has always been a challenge for many Christians. Some have to pay a high price for their courage to stand up for God. Athanasius, a fourth-century theologian and Church Father, was exiled five times by four different Roman emperors over his views against Arianism. He spent 17 of his 45 years as bishop of Alexandria in exile. Arianism declared that Christ was not the eternal Son of God but subordinate to God the Father. This view denied the Trinity where Christ was of the same substance as the Father. Athanasius was summoned by Emperor Theodosius who persuaded him to cease fighting against Arianism. "Do you realize," the emperor asked, "that all the world is against you?" Athanasius replied, "Then I am against all the world."

It is easy to succumb to group pressure. Solomon Asch conducted an experiment with a group of twelve people. They were brought into a room where two cards were on displayed. One card consisted of the reference line and the other card had three unequal lines but one of the lines had the same length as the line on the other card. The person had to choose from the second card the line that matched in length with the other line in the first card. The choice was simple enough. The first eleven persons chose the wrong line because they had been told to do so in advance. The last person who did not know about this setup was puzzled by the choice of the other eleven persons. He had to decide whether to follow the crowd or to go with what his eyes told me. Thirty-seven percent of the participants chose to follow the crowd despite what they saw with their own eyes.

Sacrifice of a Broken Spirit

"The sacrifices of God are a broken spirit; a broken and contrite heart, O God, you will not despise" (Ps 51:17). This psalm was written by David when his adulterous affair with Bathsheba was confronted by the prophet Nathan. In an unguarded moment, David fell into sin when he was walking around enjoying the evening air on the roof of his palace. There he saw Bathsheba bathing and was infatuated with her. He plotted to have her for himself by taking the life of Uriah the Hittite. The sins of David were grave. He had to bear the consequences of the choice he made. He thought he could hide this thing from others but God knew and he sent his prophet to condemn the king. "You are the man!" the prophet rebuked him. David knew that he could do nothing to atone his guilt before God. No sacrifices would wipe away his sins. The only way was to repent and admit his guilt before God. God would only accept a broken and contrite heart. In other words, David must grieve for his sins in true repentance.

It is not easy for us to face our wrongs and admit our guilt. We want to minimize the problem by thinking that it is not that serious. We rationalize the problem away or blame others for the wrongs we have committed. We will try all means to avoid the shame and pain of facing our own guilt. We are too proud to admit our sins. But the guilt will not go away. It will stay lodged in our hearts. Unrepentant sins sour our relationship with God and with the people around us. We stop growing socially, emotionally, and spiritually. A repentant heart is contrite and broken. Sin is not the only means God can use to break us. Loss, pain, and grief can also be used by God to break our hearts. A seed needs to be broken before a new life begins to emerge.

In the wilderness, Moses used a rod to shatter a rock before water flowed out to quench the thirst of the people of Israel. Jesus' body was broken at the cross before new life flowed out of him. This brokenness was commemorated in the breaking of bread with his disciples on the night he was betrayed. He broke the bread and said, "This is my body, which is for you; do this in remembrance of me" (1 Cor 11:24). He offered this new life to the Samaritan at the well. Jesus told her that the water she drew from the well would make her thirsty again. Whoever drank the water given by him would never thirst for "the water I give him will become in him a spring of water welling up to eternal life" (John 4:13–14). A "thorn" was given to Paul to torment him. The power of God flowed out of his broken life to touch the hearts of many people. "Therefore," Paul says, "I will boast all the more gladly about my weaknesses, so that Christ's power may rest on me . . . for when I am weak, then I am strong" (2 Cor 12:9–10). Our life, like the alabaster jar of perfume, when broken fills the whole house with fragrance (John 12:3). We now know why God adores a broken and humble heart.

Sacrificial Giving

Giving is not an option for Christians who see themselves as members of Christ's Body. We give in response to the grace of God displayed on the cross. God's generosity by paying a high price for our sins should inspire us to give out of thankfulness to him. Paul lays down some principles of Christian giving. We must give cheerfully and not under compulsion. We give willingly in proportion to our means. Our giving contributes to the equality and unity of the body of Christ. What does Paul mean by "equality"? It does not mean that all will receive the same amount of money or assets. It means that giving by those who have plenty will address the need of those who have needs. In this way, the gift of giving does contribute to the unity of the Church Body as well. True giving is sacrificial. If it does not hurt us to give then we have not given enough. Many Christians give a token amount out of their plenty to God. They give out the scraps or leftovers from the table. Such giving is usually not planned ahead and is ad hoc. It is a known fact that those who earn more give less. When our income increases our percentage of giving on our income decreases. Generally speaking, poorer Christians who cannot afford to give are the more generous ones.

The Sacrificial Life

The treasury was housed at the Court of the Women inside Jerusalem's Temple. The women were allowed to congregate at this place but they could not proceed further unless for sacrificial purposes. Jesus spent his time teaching and having discourse with the common people at the Court of the Women. There were 13 trumpet-shaped chests for charitable donations at the treasury. The chests were narrow at the opening and broad at the bottom. If a large amount of coins were poured into the mouth of the chest, they would get stuck at the narrow opening. The chest had to be shaken vigorously in order for the coins to pass through the narrow opening. The noise from the shaking would catch the attention of the onlookers. Of course those who put in lots of coins would attract the most attention. As for the poor widow, her two very small copper coins would go unnoticed. But Jesus noticed the widow and commented her saying:

> I tell you the truth, this poor widow has put in more than the others. All these people gave their gifts out of their wealth; but she out of her poverty put in all she had to live on (Luke 21:3–4).

Paul also commented the Macedonian Christians for their sacrificial offerings. The Macedonian Christians gave generously even though they lived in extreme poverty and were facing some severe trials. They gave beyond the ability and even pleaded with Paul to allow them in share in this joy of giving. Paul was using the example of the Macedonian Christians' rich generosity to stimulate the giving of the Corinthian church.

We Do Best by Giving

In his book, *Run with the Horses*, Eugene Peterson recalls how he saw some birds teaching their young to fly. Three young swallows were perched on a dead branch that stretched out over a lake. An adult swallow began pushing the chicks out of the end of the branch. The first one fell and started to stretch its wings and began flying on its own. The second chick did the same. The third chick was stubborn and not willing to let go of the branch. He momentarily lost its grip and then tightened again but this time hanging downwards. The parent kept pecking at his clinging talons until he had to let go of the branch. The grip was released and the wings began flapping. He was able to fly! The adult swallow had no fear that the young chick would not fly. There was no danger because birds were designed to fly. Peterson writes,

> Birds have feet and can walk. Birds have talons and can grasp a branch securely. They can walk; they can cling. But flying is their characteristic action and not until they fly are they living at their best, gracefully and beautifully. Giving is what we do best. It is the air into which we were born. It is the action that was designed into us before our birth. Some people try desperately to hold on to themselves, to live for self. They look so bedraggled and pathetic doing it, hanging on to the dead branch of selfishness and self-centeredness, afraid to risk themselves on the untried wings of giving. Yet many people don't think they can live generously because they have never tried.[5]

Costly Service

Like giving, service to God is not an option for Christian who has gained forgiveness through the blood of Jesus Christ (Heb 9:14). Every Christian is called to serve. We serve with gladness and gratitude because of what great things he has done for us (I Sam 12:24). Serving is not easy. It is hard labor that often tests our patience and resolve. "To this end," Paul writes, "I labor, struggling with all his energy, which so powerfully works in me" (Col 1:29). Paul, at times, agonized in his labor to the point of exhaustion. At one time Jesus was so exhausted ministering to the crowds that he slept throughout a storm! We can get easily discouraged and exhausted to the point of burning out unless God's power is working in us. We may not see the results immediately when we serve

---

5. Peterson, *Run With the Horses*, No page found..

God. We should not let results bother us while we do the work of the Lord. Instead, we should stand firm and let nothing affect us. Paul writes: "Always give yourselves fully to the work of the Lord, because you know that your labor in the Lord is not in vain" (1 Cor 15:58). God will not forget our labor of love when we serve him (Heb 6:10). When things are not going our way we should not give up but to continue on looking to God for sustenance and help. We should, as Paul says, stand firm and let nothing move us. We have to pay a price for our service to God. Service that costs nothing will accomplish nothing.[6]

To Care and Not to Care

Servants of God have to be careful. They have the tendency to put on a messianic complex when they over-commit and over-extend themselves in the work. They find it hard to say No to the heavy demands and succumb to the neurosis of being wanted by others all the time. They must overcome their own compulsive need to be needed. This neglect will create havoc in their spiritual lives and burn-out is common among servants of God. We can take a cue from *The Giving Tree*. Thomas Merton once said, "A tree gives glory to God first of all by being a tree." If the tree dismembers itself by constantly giving, it will end up to be just a stump, good for nothing. A stump is not exactly a tree. The best a tree can give and still remain a tree is to provide silence and shade to those who need it. "In giving less of themselves," as Belden Lane puts it, "such ministers are able to offer more than was expected."[7] This lesson is taken from another tree story. This tale was told by a Taoist monk, Chuang Tzu, in the fourth century before Christ.

One day a sage stumbled on a large and extraordinary tree located on a bare hill. He was wondering to himself what kind of a tree was that. The tree could be cut down for timber. The fact that it was still standing was because its twisted and crooked branches

---

6. Whitney, *Spiritual Disciplines for the Christian Life*, 126.
7. Lane, "The Tree as Giver of Life" 21,

were not suitable for timber. He broke a twig and tasted its sap. It was sharp and bitter. The tree was useless for tapping and not able to produce any good syrup. The leaves gave an offensive odor and too fragile to be used for mats or baskets. The roots were so gnarled and knotty that no decorative piece could be carved out of them. The sage, at last, commented after a careful examination of the tree,

> This, indeed, is a tree good for nothing. That is why it has reached so great an age. The cinnamon tree can be eaten, so it is cut down. The varnish tree is useful and therefore incisions are made of it. We all know the advantage of being useful, but only this tree knows the advantage of being useless.

The sage sat in the shade of the tree and felt the breeze blowing from the valley below. He enjoyed the scent of distant peach blossoms. While sitting in silence he happily contemplated his own uselessness.[8]

Those we serve God need to take heed of the lessons from *The Giving Tree* and *The Useless Tree*. Like the *Giving Tree*, we serve out of a compassionate heart, ready to make sacrifices when needed. To protect ourselves from fostering unhealthy dependency we must be like the *Useless Tree*. There were times Jesus avoided the crowds even though they were looking out for him. He did not want to make himself indispensable to the people around him. He took time out away from the glare of publicity and be alone by himself even when he had a busy schedule. There is a place for us to care and not to care if we want to keep our sanity and balance in our service for God.

One day a hunter found Father Anthony, one of the desert fathers, relaxing and resting with the other monks. He expressed disapproval thinking that the monks should busy themselves with prayer and work. Anthony told the hunter to put an arrow in his bow and shoot. The hunter followed his advice. The monk asked him to keep shooting and each time shoot the arrow as far as it

---

8. Lane, "The Tree as Giver of Life, 19. Adapted from a poem in David R. Brower's book, *Of All Things Most Yielding*. Friends of the Earth, no date.

The Sacrificial Life

took. The hunter protested thinking that it would break the bow when it was stretched to its limit. "So it is with the work of God," the Father said, "If we push ourselves beyond measure, the brethren will collapse. It is right, therefore, from time to time, to relax their efforts."[9]

The Cross symbolizes suffering and sacrifice. We, who carry the name of Christ, are called to live sacrificially. Peter reminds us that suffering, in different forms, is part and parcel of Christian living. The reason is simple: we do not belong in this world. The world will reject us as they had rejected our Lord. For Peter, to participate in the suffering of Christ is a joyful and blessed thing for the Christian (1 Pet 4:13–14). They are many ways we can life sacrificially for the Lord. We begin by offering parts of our bodies as instruments of righteousness to glorify him. This is not easy because the world will entice us to use them for our own gratification. In order to do this, we must learn not to bow down and succumb to the pattern of this world. Sometimes God uses pain and grief to break our hearts in order that he can use us for his glory. We must learn to yield ourselves, like the clay in the potter's hand, to God trusting that he knows what is best for us. Sacrificial giving of our hard earned money is another way for us to live sacrificially. Like giving, service to God is not an option for us. Giving and service should be exercised out of our gratitude to God who has forgiven us through the shed blood of Christ. For those who serve God, it is important to strike a balance between our zeal to serve and our need to withdraw from service in order to protect our own vocational health.

---

9. Merton, *The Wisdom of the Desert*, 63.

5

The Reviewed Life

The unexamined life is not worth living.
—SOCRATES

Burdensome Memories

SOME FRIENDS AND I went to the Botanical Gardens for a hike up a small hill. We met at the gate of the Gardens. As we were walking I noticed an old tree that was cut down and left only the stump. I heard that during a rainstorm a branch from the tree fell and hit an old man sitting under it. Unfortunately, the man did not survive the accident. The stump still looked good and solid to my eyes. It was a pity that the City Council had to cut it down to prevent any further mishaps. I saw rings on it when I looked closely at the stump. The tree could be at least seventy years old by counting the number of rings on it. The history of a tree is locked in its rings. By examining its rings we are able to know the life history of a tree: the weather conditions it endured, the periods of growth and stagnation, the times when it was afflicted with diseases, drought, fire, floods, and seasons of scarcity and abundance. We can look at the "rings" of our life in order to understand our personal history. Like trees, our personal story is filled with a dark past of failures, weaknesses, regrets, sorrows, disappointments, betrayal, and also times of joy, happiness, purpose, and fulfillment. It is not easy for us to face the truth of ourselves. We rather hide the past for fear that it will haunt us in the present. We prefer to bury our past under layers of indifferent forgetfulness because our memories can be burdensome. W. Somerset Maugham, a British playwright and novelist, wrote: "What makes old age hard to bear is not the failing of one's faculties, mental and physical, but the burden of one's memories."[1]

Though we are reluctant to dredge up the past, it is necessary for us to go back to our dark past in order to be transformed inwardly. A story is told of Nasrudin who realized that he had lost the key to the house when approaching the door of his house one night. He looked around but the night was so dark he could not even see the ground around him. He went down on his hands and knees to search for the key but it was too dark for him to find it. He again began searching for it after moving toward a street lamp. Someone came and asked him what he was doing. "I am searching for my key to the house." The person joined in the search for the missing key. After searching for a while, he asked Nasrudin whether he remembered where he lost his key. "Certainly," he replied, "I lost it in my house." "Then why are you looking for it out here," the person replied in astonishment. Nasrudin replied, "Because the light is so much better here!" Most of us prefer looking for the missing key on the outside which is easier to search. They key in fact is found inside our dark past.[2]

Embracing the Past

We know that our history has a powerful influence on the present and we need to go back to the past in order to move forward.

---

1. Chittister, *The Gift of Years,* 153. Cited W. Somerset Maugham.
2. Benner, *The Gift of Being Yourself,* 58–59.

Perhaps this was the reason why the great Church Father Augustine wrote his famous *Confessions*. In the *Confessions*, which is an autobiographical sketch of his life, Augustine was able to trace the grace of God at work throughout his past life. Augustine never took his mother's faith seriously even though he had a godly mother in Monica. His difficulties with the Christian faith were based on two issues: the inelegant writings of the Bible and the origin of evil. From a rhetorical point of view, the Bible was an inferior piece of literary work. Its language did not follow the rules of style and it contained crude stories of violence and deceit. Augustine always had difficulty over the source of evil. If God was wise and good, as claimed by Monica, then he could not have created an evil world. He began to chart his own destiny lured by his personal ambition to be a rhetorician. He never doubted his own ability in achieving his personal goals.

His life took a turn when he heard a children's voice calling on him to "take up and read." When he took up the manuscript which he had put on a nearby bench to read, the words of Paul pricked his heart: "Not in orgies and drunkenness, not in sexual immorality and debauchery, not in dissension and jealousy. Rather, clothe yourselves with the Lord Jesus Christ, and do not think about how to gratify the desires of the sinful nature" (Rom 13:13–14). Through many encounters, God turned him from a self-centered ambitious young man who loved to possess wealth, status, love, and wisdom to that of a God-fearing person. His conversion involved letting go and cease using "the beautiful things of this world" for his own narrow purposes. Instead, he directed his desires to God himself, who is the source of true beauty.[3]

Remorse and Nostalgia

Understanding our personal story by reviewing our past has its dangers. Looking back may fill us with remorse and nostalgia.[4]

---

3. Wright, "Memories of Now" 10.
4. Wright, "Memories of Now" 8.

Unearthing the past can stir up feelings of bitterness, regret, and guilt. Past hurts, bitterness, and anger still reside in our hearts at the present time. We feel remorseful when we are not able to embrace the past and not willing to let it go through forgiving ourselves and others. Forgiveness will set us free from the prison of guilt and remorse. It will not let us forget the past. It will let us remember the past in a new way. In this way, past memories no longer inhibit the present but provide hope for the future. President Bill Clinton once asked Nelson Mandela how he was able to forgive those who had kept him in prison for so long and deprived him of his basic freedom. His reply was simple: "I do not want to be in prison anymore." For those who cannot forgive, the past is often used as an excuse for everything that goes wrong in their lives. They feel strongly that their present misfortune is due to what had happened to them in the past. I know of a person who blames her parents for sending her to the wrong college. She thinks that if she had gone to the right college she will be able to get the job she wants.

In remembering we also need to stay away from romanticizing the past. Nostalgia keeps us going back to the past events and to find comfort in them. Nostalgia wants us to believe in the good things and forget the bad things at the same time. We remember fondly the beautiful roses we planted but forget the sweat and toil required to own a rose patch in the garden. We remember enjoying the fruits from the mango tree at the back of the house but forget that we had to rake the leaves at regular intervals. We remember playing with Shepherd, our pet dog, but forget the worries we had looking for her when she went missing. It is an escape to the past in order to avoid the pains of the present. The past no longer connects with the present. Instead of taking hold of the present and moving forward to face the future, we take refuge in the past. This happens to many old people who bemoan the present conditions and love to talk about the past. Joan Chittister in *The Gift of Years* writes:

> Memory is not meant to cement us in times past. It is meant to enable us to do better now that which we did not do as well before. It is the greatest teacher of them all.

> The task is to come to the point where we can trust our
> memories to guide us out of the past into a better future.[5]

Handling the Past

We are familiar with the story of Joseph in the Bible. He had a difficult past. He was betrayed by his siblings, sold as a slave to Egypt, falsely accused by his boss's wife, sent to prison, and forgotten by the man he helped to release from prison. Yet, when Joseph faced his past life there was no remorse or nostalgia. The secret lied in Joseph's willingness to forgive and be thankful for all that had happened to his life. Joseph was grateful because he could see the grace of God at work in his life. He forgave his brothers when he said to them:

> Do not be distressed and do not be angry with yourselves for selling me here, because it was to save lives that God sent me ahead of you. For two years now there has been famine in the land, and for the next five years there will not be plowing and reaping. But God sent me ahead of you to preserve for you a remnant on earth and to save your lives by a great deliverance. So then, it was not you who sent me here, but God (Gen 45:5–8).

Telling Our Stories

Remembering makes us who we are. When we look back over the course of our life, with its disappointments, pain, delights, and victories, we begin to develop a self-awareness that can lead to a transformation of our souls. Telling our stories can lead to our own conversion and is life-giving. We tell our stories in order to live. Martin Buber, who taught philosophy at Hebrew University in Jerusalem, once wrote about a rabbi who told the following story:

> My grandfather was lame. Once they asked him to tell a story about his teacher. And he related how the holy

---

5. Chittister, *The Gift of Years*, 155–56.

> Baal Shem used to hop and dance while he prayed. My grandfather rose as he spoke, and he was so swept away by his story that he himself began to hop and dance to show how the master had done. From that hour on he was cured of his lameness. That's the way to tell a story![6]

Richard Foster at one time felt that his past had impeded the glow of God's grace in his life and work. He decided to review his life history and later shared with a trusted friend over what he had discovered. He divided his life story into three phases: childhood, adolescence, and adulthood. For each period he would spend three consecutive days reviewing his life and asking God to reveal to him anything that needed healing and forgiveness. Prayerfully, he wrote down everything that came out from his memory without analysis or judgment. He went to his friend to share with him what he had written. His friend heard him and took what he had written and shredded it into pieces. He then prayed for Foster for the healing of every hurt and sorrow he had experienced in the past. Foster came out of this with a newborn freedom and it became a turning point in his life with God.[7]

Thomas More in *A Life of Work* comments that we need to open up ourselves to others by telling our stories in order to allow any insight of ourselves to come forward. We need to find the right people to listen attentively to our stories.

> The past feels like a burden only when it is thick, solid, and unsorted. You repeat the same stories, blame the same people, and feel the same frustrations. If you can look more closely and tell the stories with new detail and insight, the past loosens up. You see it in slightly fresh ways, and it is no longer a bothersome lump of emotions. It can become lighter to carry..."[8]

The Johari Window is a psychological tool developed by Joseph Luft and Harry Ingham that helps in our self-awareness and

---

6. Kidd, "The Story-Shaped Life" 22. Cited Martin Buber, *Tales of the Hasidim, Early Masters*, v–vi.

7. Thompson, *Soul Feast*, 91–92,

8. Moore, *A Life at Work*, 56–57.

personal development. It has four quadrants. The first quadrant on the top left is the Known Self: things that we know about ourselves and others know about us. The second quadrant on the top right is the Hidden Self: things we know about ourselves that others do not know. The third quadrant at the bottom left is the Blind Self: things that others know about us that we do not know. The last quadrant at the bottom right is the Unknown Self: things that neither we nor others know about us. Self-disclosure or exposure, honest feedback along with self-discovery through interaction with team members will help us in our self-discovery by expanding the first quadrant and contracting the other quadrants.

Reviewing the Past

We often identify ourselves by what we do rather than who we are. Hence, our self-knowledge is twisted based on the perceptions of others and our own. When we begin to review our personal story, we begin to know who we truly are. God may surprise us by showing glimpses and insights about ourselves that we have not known before. The word "story" means "to know".[9] By telling or creating our own story we are able to come to a self-awareness or self-knowledge which is needful for our personal development. Augustine wrote in *Confessions*, "How can you draw close to God when you are far from your own self?" He prayed saying, "Grant, Lord, that I may know myself that I may know thee."

This happens not only at the individual or personal level. It happened at the national level as well with regards to the nation of Israel. In moving forward Israel was told not to forget her past. Her story was etched in her memory through the enactment of the Passover which was celebrated annually. In celebrating the feast, she remembered her enslaved past by Egyptian slave masters. How God, through the angel of death, spared the firstborn of every Israelite family by passing over their homes but struck down every Egyptian firstborn. She was set free and escaped imminent

---

9. Kidd, "The Story-Shaped Life" 24.

death by crossing the Red Sea and witnessed firsthand the power of God's might. Her past gave her hope for the future when she faced similar challenges on her journey forward to the Promised Land. Similarly, Joshua was asked to put up memorial stones to commemorate the crossing of the Jordan River.

> In the future when your children ask you, "What do these stones mean?" tell them that the flow of Jordan was cut off before the ark of the covenant of the Lord. When it crossed the Jordan, the waters of Jordan were cut off. These stones are to be a memorial to the people of Israel forever (Josh 4:6–7).

Knowing Ourselves

Self-knowledge can only be achieved if we are honest with our self-assessment. We need to look back at our unique story with clarity and impartially. We should not be afraid to confront our dark past and the negative emotions that attached to it. We should look at our story objectively. There is no need to put blame on anybody including ourselves. Blame is a defensive measure to avoid facing the past self. There is no need to justify or excuse our past deeds. We should look at the past in a non-judgmental and detached way.

Self-Examination[10]

In order to feel secure enough to look inside ourselves, we need to open ourselves to God who loves us and knows us. We know that we cannot escape God's scrutiny. We can hide things from others and even from ourselves, but God knows us through and through. The psalmist wrote: "You know when I sit and when I arise; you perceive my thoughts from afar, you discern my going out and my lying down; you are familiar with all my ways" (Ps 139:2–3). The psalmist's identity was forged in God's presence where he knew

---

10. Indebted to Barton for discussing self-examination using this psalm. See her book, *Sacred Rhythms*, 91–101.

that he was the focus of God's love. He was wonderfully and fearfully made when God formed his inward parts and knitted him when he was in his mother's womb (Ps 139:13-14). The ability to celebrate and accept who he was led to the disclosure of himself before God. He was no longer afraid of the darkness residing in him. He knew that he could not escape God's presence and scrutiny: "Where can I flee from your presence . . . even the darkness is not dark to you . . . for darkness is as light to you" (Ps 139:7,12). Secured in God's loving presence, the psalmist was able to disclose the dark side of his personality:

> If only you will slay the wicked, O God! Away from me, you bloodthirsty men! They speak of you with evil intent; your adversaries misuse your name. Do I not hate those who hate you, O Lord, and abhor those who rise up against you? I have nothing but hatred for them; I count them my enemies (Ps 139:19-22).

Even in the darkest part of his soul, God was there. In disclosing his deepest thoughts and feelings, he was ready to let God search him and reveal to him those things that needed to be dislodged from the hidden part of his life. He was ready to allow God to throw a spotlight on his soul in order to test and search his innermost being. The psalmist called on God: "Search me, O God, and know my heart; test me and know my anxious thoughts. See if there is any offensive way in me, and lead me in the way everlasting" (Ps 139:23-24).

Knowing Who God Is

When we invite God to search us, we begin to see ourselves in a clearer light. At the same time, as we bare our hearts in God's presence, we also take on a greater understanding of who God is. Self-knowledge and knowledge of God are intertwined. We cannot have one without the other. Calvin wrote at the beginning of his *Institutes* saying:

> Without knowledge of self there is no knowledge of God. Knowing God and self is required for us to grow and develop spiritually . . . But as these are connected together by many ties, it is not easy to determine which of the two precedes and gives birth to the other.[11]

In the vision given by God to Catherine of Siena, she was asked to imagine a garden with a circle inscribed on the ground.[12] The tree of the soul grows within this inscribed circle of good soil. In growing the soul, the gardener has to work closely at the good soil. For the tree of the soul to grow well, he needs to widen and deepen the circle at the same time. She was to imagine that the width of the circle is the knowledge of herself and the depth of the circle is her knowledge of God. We all know that we can only dig a deeper hole in the ground by widening the circle of the hole. The lesson of this vision is clear. The more we grow in self-knowledge and know who we are, the more we grow in the knowledge of God and know who God is.

Journal Writing

The spiritual discipline of journal writing will help us to keep track of our story. It records our struggles, questions, setbacks, victories, and insights. Over time we may be able to see a pattern or a bigger picture in terms of what is God doing in our lives. We are able to detect the strengths and weakness of our walk with God. In this way, journal writing is a "way of listening to oneself and to God."[13] A journal is different from a diary. A diary keeps track of the events that happen on a daily or regular basis. A journal is a record of the works and ways of God in our lives.[14] Here we want to look at the events or happenings from a spiritual perspective and to record down our feelings and thoughts about them.

11. Calvin, *Institutes of the Christian Religion*, Vol 1, 37.
12. Maricle, *Deeply Rooted*, 11
13. Thompson, *Soul Feast*, 35.
14. Whitney, *Spiritual Disciplines for the Christian Life*, 205.

Many times, David recorded his feelings and thoughts in poetic language. We find this in the book of Psalms. One dark night, David found himself looking up at the starry sky above him and was astounded by its silent majesty and beauty. Inspired and amazed by God's handiwork, he composed his thoughts in his journal: "The heavens declare the glory of God; the skies proclaim the word of his hands. Day after day they pour forth speech; night after night they display knowledge" (Ps 19:1–2). After fleeing from King Saul as a hunted fugitive, David wrote his emotions in a psalm. He endurance was reaching its limit and unless God intervened he would easily succumb to his enemies. David wrote his feelings in this psalm of lament: "How long, O Lord? Will you forget me forever? How long will you hide your face from me? How long must I wrestle with my thoughts and every day have sorrow in my heart? How long will my enemy triumph over me?" (Ps 13:1–2).

Not to Forget

Occasionally I will write down the works and ways of God in my life. I don't do this very often but I do keep track by writing down my thoughts, feelings, and reflections on my life with God. Every time when God spoke to me, or when he jolted me out of my complacency, or when something happened to me that drew me to him, I would write them down. I have been faithfully doing this over the years and this has helped my spiritual life. It is easy for me to forget. A journal will remind me of the gracious work of God in my life. I am reminded that I am God's workmanship and he is still actively working out his purpose and plan for my life. Like the psalmist, I too will say, "I will remember the deeds of the Lord; yes, I will remember your miracles of long ago. I will meditate on all your works and consider all your mighty deeds" (Ps 77:11–12).

Meet My True Self

In writing my journal, I will meet my true self. Here I will bare my innermost thoughts and feelings to God. The words come from deep down my heart and I feel that there is no barrier between him and me. I am free to express my self because I know that I am known by him more than I know myself. David Brainerd who was a missionary to the American Indians shared in his journal the despair that was lodged deep in his heart with no reservation at all.

> Lord's Day, December 16, 1744. Was so overwhelmed with dejection that I knew not how to live. I longed for death exceedingly; my soul as sunk into deep waters and the floods were ready to drown me. I was so much oppressed that my soul was in a kind of horror. I could not keep my thought fixed in prayer for the space of one minute, without fluttering and distraction. It made me exceedingly ashamed that I did not live to God.[15]

Closer to God

When I begin to review my journal, I feel closer to God and my faith in him is strengthened knowing that he has been with me all along through the ups and downs that life has offered me. He has been my guide and friend through times of despair and delight. He remains my faithful companion and a good listener to my woes and complaints. He may not always fulfill my wishes and demands, but he has been there when I need him through the twists and turns of life. Reflecting on my past I can see more clearly about who I am and who God is to me. He loves me for who I am. And through this, I too have learned to accept myself as I am. I cannot deny my past. What I am today is due to my past life. I need to embrace and accept it in order to be free from it. This allows me to move forward with hope and with great anticipation that God who

---

15. Whitney, *Spiritual Disciplines for the Christian Life*, 209. Cited Jonathan Edwards, ed., *The Life and Diary of David Brainerd*, 186.

began a good work in me will carry it on to completion until the day of Jesus Christ (Phil 1:6).

Past memories can be painful and we avoid thinking about them at the present. In order to move forward, we need to embrace our past. The past may stir up feelings of guilt and regret. Forgiveness is the key for us to overcome these feelings. There is also a tendency for us to feel nostalgic about the past. To avoid the painful present we take refuge in the past. This prevents us to take hold of the present and move forward to the future. One way to avoid this is to review our past and tell our stories to a close friend. We begin to acquire a true knowledge of ourselves when we open ourselves to others by telling our stories. Self-knowledge will lead us to know God more. This will enhance our spiritual walk with God. One way to keep a record of our past is to keep a journal. The journal will help us trace the gracious work of God in our lives. In this journal, we will write down the ways and work of God in our lives. The journal will help us review our lives when we bare our thoughts and feelings to God. When reviewing our past, we will meet our true self. At the same time, we feel closer to God knowing that he has been with us through the twists and turns of living our lives before him.

6

The Abiding Life

"However strong the branch becomes, however far away it reaches round the home, out of sight of the vine, all its beauty and all its fruitfulness ever depend upon that one point of contact where it grows out of the vine. So be it with us too."

—ANDREW MURRAY

Modular Structure of Trees

Trees are different from the other living creatures. Unlike animals, trees are immobile and cannot run away from their predators. They are under constant attacks by the herbivores. Trees, for this reason, have adopted a different strategy for survival. Their bodies are constructed on a modular basis. Unlike animals with vital organs, trees can afford to lose a limb or two without any major threat to their livelihood. Large sections of a tree can be cut off without putting it at risk. In time the tree will grow back to its normal state. Animals cannot afford to lose any part of their physiology without putting their survival at risk. The function of trees is not based on specific organs in their bodies. They breathe without lungs, eat without mouths, stand erect without bones or skeletons, and respond to outside stimuli without eyes or ears. Trees do not have brains to control the different parts of the body.

Get Connected

A tree can afford to lose a branch or branches but a branch cannot afford to be cut off from the trunk if it wants to remain strong and fruitful. In the parable of the Vine and Branches, we know that a branch can be pruned by the gardener if it wants to produce more fruit. A branch is useless unless it is connected to the trunk or vine. A useless branch will be cut off and burned. As Christians, we are the branches that need to stay connected with Christ, who is the True Vine. We first come to remain in Christ when we come to faith to him. Only Jesus can satisfy our spiritual hunger and thirst. Jesus declares, "I am the bread of life. He who comes to me will never go hungry, and he who believes in me will never be thirsty ... Whoever eats my flesh and drinks my blood remains in me and I in him" (John 6:35,56). Those who feed on the bread of life will live and have eternal life. We get connected to Jesus when we first believe in his broken body and blood to cleanse us and forgive us of our sins. The challenge is for Christians to stay connected or remain in him.

Stay Connected

To stay connected we need to build an ongoing relationship with Jesus. This requires us to remain in his love and his words remain in us (John 15:7,10). In other words, we need to look to Scripture to maintain our intimacy with God. Our relationship with God is based on his love for us. We can only respond to his love by obeying his words. Christians are encouraged to read Scripture to know more about God. We cannot relate well to another person unless we take the trouble to get to know the person well. Knowing the Bible is one thing but we can only have Jesus' words remain in us when we do what we know. Nothing will happen to our relationship with God if we do not obey what we have heard or read. "Now that you know these things, you will be blessed if you do them" (John 13:17). "Do not merely listen to the word . . . do what it says" (James 1:22).

The Transforming Word

Ruth Barton, in *Sacred Rhythms*, points out the difference between reading Scripture as a text and reading a love letter.[1] We often approach Scripture to gather information and use it to accomplish some specific purpose like preaching a sermon or conducting a Bible Study. Our primary concern, in using a text, is to use its information to gain knowledge or to help us solve a problem or meet a need. But Scripture is spiritual food that keeps us spiritually alive. The Word should transform our lives and not just a source of information only. We should read Scripture like receiving a letter from someone we love deeply. Scripture reading not only satisfies our minds but touches our hearts and emotions as well.

Reading a text is different from reading a love letter. We read a text to glean the most information in the shortest time possible. If our text is a newspaper, we will probably scan the headlines and flip through the pages to our favorite sports or entertainment page. While doing that we will look out for adverts, photos or articles that capture our interest. We come with an inquisitive mind but not a listening heart to listen to what has been written. The information we glean may not touch us at the emotional or volitional level.

The Mind of Christ

Reading a love letter is different. We will take the time to read, not once but many times, just to get to a deeper level of understanding in order to nurture and appreciate the relationship we have with

---

1. Barton, *Sacred Rhythms*, 49.

the writer. As we read we may be wondering what she or he is feeling or thinking. We may slow down and read the words again just to make sure that we understand correctly what is written. We bring along our own set of feelings and thoughts as we read the letter. It is not surprising that letters written out of a love relationship are carefully kept and preserved by the receiver for sentimental reasons. We are most willing to obey or do whatever the letter instructs us in order to please the person we love.

When Paul wrote to Philemon concerning Onesimus, his former slave, he was confident that Philemon whom he had a close relationship would do what he requested in the letter. It was a letter written out of love both for his friend Philemon and his spiritual son, Onesimus. Paul also mentioned that the appeal on behalf of Onesimus to him was made on the basis of love (Phlm 9). He wanted Philemon to reconcile with his former slave who was now a brother in the Lord. In the letter, Paul also acknowledged Philemon's love for him which caused him great joy and encouragement. "Confident of your obedience, I write to you, knowing that you will do even more than I ask" (Phlm 7, 21). Though it was not easy to receive back a runaway slave, Philemon had no reason to reject his appeal based on the love relationship he had with the apostle.

We read a text for its functional value, whereas we read Scripture, God's love letter, for its relational value. We glean information from a text, but when reading God's Word, we are spiritually informed and formed. The changes in our inner being will also affect changes to our outward behavior as well. Our personalities, social behavior, and human relationships will be affected. We will take on the mind of Christ and become more Christlike (Rom 8:5–8). We normally read Scripture for the purpose of encouragement and edification. From the biblical passage, we may want to extract some principles that we can immediately apply to our lives. We approach the Bible by asking questions: What was the background? Who were the people involved and how were they related? What was the occasion? Who were the original readers? Why did this take place? We ask these questions to get to the meaning of the passage and applying it to our lives. Reading Scripture in this manner requires the mind to be active and fully engaged.

Spiritual Reading of Scripture

There is another way of reading Scripture. It is called Spiritual Reading or *Lectio Divina*. This style of reading Scripture was practiced by Christians in the past. This style does not come to Scripture by using questions to tease it to reveal its meaning to the reader. Instead, the reader comes with an open heart to listen to "the still small voice" of God. She comes opening herself to God for him to speak to her using a word or words from the selected passage of Scripture. She reads the chosen passage of Scripture, slowly and repeatedly, not to extract information but to meet God on his own terms. She reads prayerfully with depth and receptivity. She ponders over the words and reflects on them. She is ready to receive from God, a word or phrase, that he uses to speak to her. Through this, God is drawing her into his presence and guides her to rest in him. To simply rest in God is the object of prayerfully reading the Scriptures. The practice of *Lectio Divina* involves four steps.[2]

The Practice of Lectio Divina

First, we need to choose a text that we want to pray over. Make sure our bodies are relaxed and in a comfortable position. Some deep breathing may help us to relax and focus. Allow ourselves to be silent for a time before the reading begins. Read the text slowly and reflectively. Do not hurry but let each word sinks in. After the first reading, allow a short period of silence. At the second reading, a word(s) from God may impress or catch our attention. The word(s) that resonates with us is God's gentle voice inviting us into

---

2. The material in this section is extracted from my book, *Being Human*, 85–86.

his presence. At this stage, do not continue reading but move to the second stage.

Second, ponder over the word(s) in our hearts. Meditate, memorize, or repeat the word(s) in our hearts until it speaks to our present situation. What area of our lives has the word(s) touches us? Now we know that God has used it to speak to our lives what should be our response?

Third, we need to talk to God in prayer. This dialogue with God may not necessarily be verbal. What God has awakened in our hearts, we need to offer it back to him. What is God calling us to do or become? What inner experience is God calling us to reflect on? Say the prayer of praise and thanksgiving about these things to God that arise in our hearts.

Fourth, we need to enter into a time of silence and simply rest in his presence. Experience the quiet fullness of God's love and peace in our hearts as we open ourselves to him. Jesus promises us rest as we go to him (Matt 11:28–30). The Spiritual Reading of Scripture is best summed up by Francois Fenelon:

> As to the subject of your meditations, take such passages of the Gospels or the Imitation of Christ. Read slowly, and when a passage touches you, use it as you would a sweetmeat, which you hold in your mouth till it melts. Let the meaning sink slowly into your heart, and do not pass on to something else until you feel that to be exhausted . . . Trust God simply, like a child, in telling him whatever comes to your mind. The thing is open your heart to God, to make it familiar with him, to strengthen it with love. Carefully fostered love, enlightens amends, corrects, encourages.[3]

Prayer Deepens Intimacy

While we look to Scripture to maintain and grow in our relationship with God, prayer deepens our intimacy with him. Prayer is the lifeline of our spiritual lives. Prayer, according to Henri Nouwen,

---

3. Fenelon, "A Persevering Will to Pray" 38.

is the most basic movement of the spiritual life.[4] No person hopes to stay spiritually alive without the need to pray for it is the very breath of life. It is the life sign of our faith just as breathing is a clear sign of being alive. Prayer, like the cry of a newborn baby, comes naturally to us the moment we are spiritually born. It is the first act that ushers us into God's kingdom when we become a part of Christ's Body. It is also the one act on which all our other spiritual exercises depend. Fasting is practiced in the context of prayer, while meditation leads to a prayerful response. Reading of Scripture will result in the prayer of confession. Prayer not only saturates everything we do in life but redeems every aspect of our lives as well. It is the key link in our engagement with God. Intimacy with God is not possible without prayer.

Be Still and Pray

We often view prayer as talking to God. Prayer becomes a monologue with us speaking all the time. This one-sided affair can be frustrating at times when we do not receive any feedback in return. We feel that we are speaking to a wall and we only hear the echo of our own words. We come to a point when we ask ourselves who do we actually speak to: God or us? Prayer should be two-sided. Both sides should talk to each other in order for any relationship to remain healthy and growing. Communication is key to any good relationship. Prayer requires us to listen first before we speak. We can only listen properly when we still ourselves before God in silence. Solitude (alone with God) and silence play an important role in our prayer life.[5] Our minds become uncluttered when we still ourselves before God.

Many of our prayers are actually mind-talk. Prayer is more than the activity of the mind. It involves the heart as well. It is possible that our minds are full of talk and thoughts when we pray, but our hearts are empty and far away from God. Words coming from

---

4. Nouwen, *Reaching Out*, 114.

5. See my chapter on solitude and silence in *Take Up Your Mat and Walk*, 89–102.

an empty heart sound hollow like the sound of gongs or cymbals. When we speak words out of a full heart filled with divine silence, they can be powerful and have far-reaching consequences. God spoke to create a world out of silence. We do not need to say much when we pray after a time of solitude and silence. "Much can be said without much being spoken," writes Nouwen.[6] We tend to use our minds to master the world around us. When we use our minds in our prayers there is a tendency for us to take charge. The Spirit that dwells and prays in our hearts is not given the space to take charge of our prayer life. That is the reason why the desert monks have this advice to those who want to excel in their prayer life. "The chief task of the athlete (that is, the monk) is to enter into his heart."[7] Paul reminds us of the Spirit's role in our prayer life.

> The Spirit helps us in our weakness. We do not know what we ought to pray for, but the Spirit himself intercedes for us with groans that words cannot express. And he who searches our hearts knows the mind of the Spirit, because the Spirit intercedes for the saints in accordance with God's will (Rom 8:26–7).

Children learn to speak by listening to adults around them. They gradually pick up the language skills by imitating the speech of others. This should also be the case in the development of our prayer life. We listen first before we speak. Prayer is initiated by God and when our inner spirit is touched by God's Spirit, then we are drawn to speak before him. God can speak to us using various channels. He speaks to us primarily through his Word. He also speaks to us through his creation, other people, visions, dreams, circumstances, and journal keeping.

Pruning and Bearing Fruit

One of the results of abiding in Christ is that we will bear fruit. But God wants us not just to be fruitful, but to bear more fruit for him.

---

6. Nouwen, *The Way of the Heart*, 57.
7. Nouwen, *The Way of the Heart*, 77.

The fruitless branches will be cut off and those which bear fruit God prunes so that they will be even more fruitful (John 15:2). This means that we will subject ourselves to be pruned by God.[8] Pruning also gets rid of those unwanted branches that are dead or diseased. It keeps the plant in a better shape as well. Pruning is not easy for the gardener because he has watched the plant grows over time from tiny twigs to full branches. It is daunting for him but the job needs to be done in order to produce bigger blossoms and more fruit. God will bring situations into our lives that can be painful but necessary for our spiritual development and growth. Every saint of God can testify to this. God may want us to let go of something or someone that we hold dear to our hearts. It is painful to let go. Conversely, God may want us to accept a situation or person that we may not like. It is equally painful to accept the unpleasant.

Taming the Heart

The Puritans of the seventeenth century believed that afflictions were used by God to tame the heart. To Richard Baxter, a famous Puritan pastor, the heart is like "an untamed colt not used to the hand."[9] The Puritans were farmers who were tied to the soil. Being farmers, they were able to discern God's disciplinary hand in the natural world around them. Living in an enchanted world, they were filled with awe and wonder at the creation of God. They were, at the same time, terrified by the disturbances of the natural forces around them. To them, the inner chaos associated with the spiritual life was like the raging sea. Weathering the storms of life was a prelude to a purified desire for God. They took seriously Paul's words saying that Christians must go through many hardships to enter the kingdom of God (Acts 14:22). Hardships were occasions used by God to cleanse their souls, purify their faith, and strengthen their relationship with him. Their uncontrolled pas-

---

8. The material in this section on pruning is extracted from my book, *Garden of the Soul*, 29–30, 57–8.

9. Baxter, *The Saints' Everlasting Rest*, 147.

sions were now curbed and channeled to good use. They were able to extinguish their affections and to wean them from the earthly things of life.

Anne Bradstreet compared God's use of affliction to a mother's weaning her baby by rubbing wormwood or mustard on her breast. Knowing how easily she could fall in love with the world and be dependent on it for earthly joys, she lamented saying, "I have found by experience, I can no more live without correction than without food."[10] She took delight in difficulties because every affliction that brought chaos to her life revealed God's love and power that could wean her from earthly attachments. Samuel Rutherford, a Scottish theologian and author, shared the same sentiment. He said, "When I am in the cellar of affliction, I look for the Lord's choicest wine."[11] Only the best fruits make the choicest wine.

What Does it Mean to be Fruitful?

A Christlike Character

What does it mean to be fruitful? It usually means to bear a Christlike life. When we are attached to Christ, we begin to take upon us the characteristics that we see in Christ. "But the fruit of the Spirit," Paul says, "is love, joy, peace, patience, kindness, goodness, faithfulness, gentleness, and self-control" (Gal 5:22–23). We cannot produce these virtues through our own effort. They come naturally when we are in a close relationship with Christ. So our focus is not to be more loving or kind but to remain close to Jesus at all times. This is made possible when we obey God out of love for him, pray as a mark of our dependence on him, and submit ourselves to his loving hand to prune us.

---

10. Backstreet, *The Works of Anne Backstreet*, 38. Cited by Lane, *Ravished by Beauty*, 145.

11. Lane, *Ravished by Beauty*, 146.

Good Deeds

We also bear fruit when we do good deeds. Paul prayed for the Colossian Church that they might bear fruit in every good work and grow in the knowledge of God as they walked worthy of the Lord (Col 1:10). The more we know God and his love, the more we are capable of doing good works before people. Good deeds also involve giving away money to help the less fortunate. Paul considered the money given to the Jerusalem Church as fruit. "So after I have completed this task and have made sure that they have received this fruit, I will go to Spain and visit you on the way" (Rom 15:28). Jesus also talked about Christians letting their light shine before men that they might see their good deeds and praise the Father in heaven (Matt 5:16). To be able to do good to others out of Christ's love is a sign that we are abiding in Jesus. Thomson writes:

> When we abide in the vine of Jesus' life, a single vital sap runs through us. This sap is a love that pours itself out for others. Jesus gives us everything he has and is. To abide in him is to participate in that outpouring of love.[12]

Converts for God

To bear fruit is to win souls for the Kingdom of God. Paul considered the conversion of the household of Stephanas as the first fruits of Achaia (1 Cor 16:15). Paul also longed to go to Rome in order to reap a harvest of souls there (Rom 1:13). He also considered his Gospel work in Philippi as fruitful labor (Phil 1:22). Fruitfulness will also result in praise and thanksgiving to God. The author to Hebrews called on Christians to continually offer to God a sacrifice of praise—the fruit of lips that confess his name (Heb 13:15).

---

12. Thompson, *Soul Feast*, 39.

Answered Prayers

Another result of abiding in Christ is answered prayer. The Bible says, "If you remain in me and my words remain in you, ask whatever you wish, and it will be given you" (John 15:7). We all know that our prayers often go unanswered. A story is told of a boy who found a cigar. He quietly went to an alley and lit it up. While he was enjoying his first taste of cigar, he saw his dad coming his way. He quickly hid his cigar behind his back and acting casual. To create a diversion, he pointed to a billboard and asked his dad, "Can we go to the circus this weekend?" His dad, looking straight at his face, said quietly, "Never make a petition while at the same time trying to hide a smoldering disobedience!"

There are two conditions attached to this promise of answered prayers. Can it be that our prayers are unanswered because these two conditions are not met? The first is to make sure that we abide or remain in Christ. We know what it takes to remain in Christ. The second is that Christ's words remain in us. It means for us to take God's words to heart, to know them well, and to obey them. When we do, we have aligned our will to God's will. God's desires become our desires and we only want what God wants. We are then able to delight in whatever God is doing. When we do that he will grant us the desires of our hearts (Ps 37:4).

Keep Sin at Bay

"No one who lives in him keeps on sinning," proclaimed the apostle John (1 John 3:6). If we remain in Christ we will keep sin at bay. This does not mean that we cannot sin. It means the grip of sin on our lives is no longer strong. At the same time, we will not be ashamed or fearful at the coming of our Lord. Instead, if we continue in him we will arm ourselves with confidence before him at his coming (1 John 2:28).

Be Strong in the Lord

Branches are strong only if they are closely attached to the trunk. The weight of the leaves which the branches carry is not heavy. When they are soaked with rainwater, covered with snow, or hit by strong winds, the strength of the branches will be severely tested due to the increase in weight. Where does our strength come from when we are severely tested in our faith? Paul believes that God is the source of our strength. He exhorts us to be strong in the Lord and in his mighty power (Eph 6:10). We remain strong as long as we are connected and tapped into this source. Our strength comes through the Holy Spirit who dwells in us. Paul's prayer for the Ephesian Christians was that "out of his glorious riches he may strengthen you with power through his Spirit in your inner being, so that Christ may dwell in you in your hearts through faith" (Eph 3:16–7). Our strength does not come from ourselves but from the grace of God (2 Tim 2:1).

Sometimes, this strength in the inner being is veiled in weakness. When we are weak and look to God for strength, then we are strong. Paul's thorn in the flesh is a good example. We do not know what exactly was this thorn. Was it a sickness or a physical disability? Apparently, Paul did not like it because he considered it a weakness. It was sent to torment Paul in order to keep him from becoming proud due to the special revelations he received from God. Nevertheless, Paul recognized its usefulness and accepted it as from God. God spoke to Paul saying, "My grace is sufficient for you, for my power is made perfect in weakness" (2 Cor 12:9).

The key to our spiritual growth and development is to maintain a close relationship with Christ. We get connected when we believe in Jesus and become a member of his Body. To stay connected is a big challenge for many Christians. The reading of Scripture with the goal of obeying his words is the place to begin. Our obedience is a testimony of our love for our Lord. Intimacy is further deepened through prayer. Prayer requires us to listen first before we talk. It is not an easy task because we always think that prayer is talking to God. We can learn to listen well through the ancient practice of *Lectio Divina*, the Spiritual Reading of Scripture. The result of abiding in Christ is to live a fruitful life for him. Many times, God will bring adverse situations into our lives to prune us in order that we bear even more fruit. To be fruitful means that we adopt a Christlike character, perform good deeds for those in needs, bring others to believe in Christ and know him, see our prayers answered by God to the delight of our souls, and living a life free from the grip of sin. Afflictions are used by God to tame our souls so that in our "weakness" we can be strong for him. We remain strong as long as we stay connected and tapped into the power of the Holy Spirit who dwells in us. Our strength comes from God's grace and not from ourselves.

7

The Rejuvenated Life

The desert and the parched land will be glad;
the wilderness will rejoice and blossom.
Like the crocus, it will burst into bloom;
it will rejoice greatly and shout for joy . . .
The burning sand will become a pool,
the thirsty ground bubbling springs

—Is 35:1,7

The Greening of Kubuji Desert

THE ONLY WAY TO hold back desertification is the planting of shrubs and trees. This happens to the Kubuji desert in Inner Mongolia.[1] It has an area of around 18,600 square kilometers of golden sand dunes with a population of about 740,000. In the past, people lived poorly due to the aridity of land. In 1988, a private Chinese company decided to change things in the area. Locals were recruited to plant trees and shrubs. After decades of experi-

---

1. http://time.com/4851013/china-greening-kubuqi-desert-land-restoration/ July 27, 2017. Charlie Campbell/Baotou.

mentation with different techniques and various types of plants and trees, the hard work is paying off. More than a third of the Kubuji has been greened. Special drought-resistant plants have been used to grip the shifting sand dunes from encroaching on the farms and villages. Locals are encouraged to plant licorice which does not require much water and can be sold for a profit. Licorice is used extensively in TCM (traditional Chinese medicine). The livelihood of the local people has improved. Meng, who used to own two hundred sheep, has seen his flock expanded to seven hundred sheep and eighty cows. The leaves of plants play an influential role in the weather of the area. In a forested area, the rain trapped by the leaves does not splash heavily on the soil below resulting in small streams of flowing water. A lot of water is drained away quickly and wasted. Instead, the water is collected and absorbed by the soft soil when it drips slowly to the ground. Water is retained in this manner and the land is refreshed and rejuvenated. As the dry land needs water, so our soul, which at times can be dry and thirsty, needs the refreshment of the Spirit of God in order for us to remain spiritually healthy and growing.

Hitting a Dry Patch

Most of us, from time to time, have gone through a dry patch in our spiritual lives. We know we are going through a spiritual drought in our lives when we begin to lose interest in the things of God or feel that God has abandoned us altogether. We begin to cast doubts on our faith and focus on our failures. We get irritable and impatient with ourselves and with the people around us. We question our work and wonder whether it is worth the effort after all. We lack the passion in spiritual matters and making excuses for our spiritual lapses. W.E. Sangster, a gifted Methodist preacher, wrote about the things that impacted him badly when he was going through a dry patch in his spiritual life:

> I am a minister of God, and yet my private life is a failure in these ways: a) I am irritable and easily put out; b) I am impatient with my wife and children; c) I am deceitful

in that I often express private annoyance when a caller is announced and simulate pleasure when I actually greet them; d) From the examination of my heart, I conclude that most of my study has been crudely ambitious: that I wanted degrees more than knowledge and praise rather than equipment for service; e) Even in my preaching I fear that I am more often wondering what people think of me, than what they think about my Lord and His word; f) I have long felt in a vague way, that something was hindering the effectiveness of my ministry and I must conclude that the "something" is my failure in living the truly Christian life; g) I am driven in pain to conclude that the girl who has lived as a maid in my house for more than three years has not felt drawn to the Christian life because of me; h) I find slight envies in my heart at the greater success of other young ministers. I seem to match myself with them in thought and am vaguely jealous when they attract more notice than I do.[2]

Running Empty

There are many reasons why we experience a dryness in our souls. One of the reasons is due to the physical and emotional exhaustion that affect our spiritual lives. Elijah started well. He confronted the Baal worshipers on Mount Carmel and had a great victory. He was alone confronting the hundreds of Baal worshipers. Elijah gave his all for God and he was drained of his physical and emotional energy after the confrontation. He might not realize his own condition. After the triumphant effort, he became vulnerable. The threat posed by Queen Jezebel triggered an emotional and psychological meltdown in the prophet. He took the threat seriously. He became afraid and ran for his own life. He went a day's journey into the desert from Beersheba, the southernmost point of Israel. Sitting under a broom tree, he prayed that he might die. "Take my life; I am no better than my ancestors" (1 Kgs 19:4). Shortly, Elijah fell asleep due to exhaustion and fatigue. An angel came and

---

2. Sangster, *Doctor Sangster*, 90. Cited by MacDonald, *Restoring Your Spiritual Passion*, 49–50.

ministered to him with bread and water. The prophet was running on an empty tank and what he needed was to refill the tank. Often times, we experience burnout or exhaustion because we do not take time out of a busy and stressful schedule. We spend so much time attending to God's work that we have given ourselves little space and time to attend to our needs. Elijah's zeal for God and his work was influenced by the perception that he was the only prophet left in Israel to fight the Lord's battles.

> I have been been very zealous for the Lord God Almighty. The Israelites have rejected our covenant, broken down your altars, and put your prophets to death with the sword. I am the only one left, and now they are trying to kill me" (1 Kgs 19:10).

Failure is not Bad

When we are spiritually dry, we sometimes conclude that we are not up to the task God has given us and we have failed. Elijah felt that he had failed God. The victory at Mount Carmel was momentary and did not change the spiritual outlook of the nation. Jezebel was not moved and Ahab's enthusiasm was short-lived. He did nothing to change the spiritual status quo of the nation. Failures or wounds in our lives may not necessarily be bad. They can be the source of our greatest gifts if we learn well from them.[3] "We grow spiritually much more by doing it wrong than by doing it right," says Richard Rohr.[4]

A story was told by a Sufi master to his student when he came to him for advice. The student told him that he had done terrible things in his life and he knew that God could never forgive him. What could he do? "Ah, my son," the master replied, "Don't you see? All of us are connected to God by a piece of rope that is the same length for every one of us. When we sin, alas, we cut the rope that connects us to the Holy One. But when we repent, God

---

3. Lane, *Backpacking with the Saints*, 137.
4. Rohr, *Falling Upward*, xxii. Cited by Lane, *Backpacking*, 137.

is eager to tie the pieces together again. Every time you tie a knot in a rope, of course, it gets shorter. Hence, those with more knots in their rope are that much closer to God. So trust, my son, in the forgiveness of God, the Merciful and Compassionate One. He loves to tie knots!"[5]

Struggling with Sin

Another reason that we experience spiritual dryness is due to sin in our lives. King David is a good example. David was not leading in battle and he had some spare time at hand. While walking on the roof of his palace he noticed Bathsheba bathing and was attracted to her beauty. We all know the rest of the story. In order to hide his adulterous affair with Bathsheba, he killed Uriah, her husband. David had all these undercover until he was confronted by the prophet, Nathan. He could no longer hide his sin any longer. He confessed and repented of his sins before God. "I know my transgressions," David wrote, "and my sin is always before me. Against you, you only, have I sinned and done what is evil in your sight" (Ps 51:3–4). Though David could hide his sins from others, he could not hide them from himself. He was continually reminded of his wrongdoings. His guilt haunted him all day long and he carried with it wherever he went. He felt it in his spirit and bones. He pleaded to God saying, "Let me hear joy and gladness; let the bones you have crushed rejoice" (Ps 51:8). Joy and gladness left him. He had quenched the Holy Spirit and he could not feel God's presence in his life (Ps 51:11). He asked God to forgive and restore him back to fellowship again. "Restore to me the joy of salvation and grant me a willing spirit, to sustain me" (Ps 51:12).

Confession of Sin

We experience a spiritual famine in our lives when we sin. Sin separates us from God. He hides his face from us and he will not

5. Cited by Lane, *Backpacking*, 137–38.

hear our prayers (Is 59:2). God withholds his Spirit from us and we lose the joy of salvation. Confession is the only way out of this spiritual famine. Failure to confess will weaken our lives spiritually, emotionally and physically. "When I keep silent," David said, "my bones wasted away through my groaning all day long. For day and night your hand was heavy upon me; my strength was sapped as in the heat of summer" (Ps 32:4–5). Confession means "to speak the same thing." When we confess we are agreeing with God as to what is wrong with us. When we confess our sins before the Lord he will forgive the guilt of our sins. We will receive back the joy of salvation and our relationship with him is restored (Ps 51:12).

A young monk stole a valuable Bible from the cell of Abba Gelasius and took it to a bookseller and asked how much money he could get from selling the Bible. The bookseller told him that he would ask around and get back to him. When the monk returned some time later the bookseller explained that he had consulted Abba Gelasius since he was the best person to ask concerning the value of the Bible. The Abba said that he could sell it for no less than 18 pieces of silver since it was a valuable Bible. The young monk asked whether it was all that he had said. He also wanted to know whether the Abba asked who was selling it. The bookseller replied saying that the Abba did not say anything. The young monk then took the Bible back to the monastery and gave it back to Abba Gelasius. He had found something more precious than the Bible. He had found forgiveness.[6] "If we confess our sins," John says, "he is faithful and just to forgive us our sins and purify us from all unrighteousness" (1 John 1:9). The door to the spiritual healing of our souls is through confession. Bernard of Clairvaux, best known for the great hymn "Jesus the very thought of Thee," had this to say about the power of confession:

> How often, when I have poured out my grief and shame, hast Thou anointed my sore conscience with Thy mercy and poured the oil of gladness on my wounds! How often has the prayer that I began, almost despairing of salvation, sent me back full of joy and confident of pardon!

---

6. Ward, *Sayings of the Desert Fathers*, 446.

> Those in like case know well that the Lord Jesus is a Doctor who heals the contrite-hearted and remedies their sickness. Those who lack this experience, let them believe His own words when he says, "Thou Lord hath anointed me to preach good tidings to the meek, to bind the brokenhearted." Let them come and prove him for themselves, that they may learn the meaning of saying, "I will have mercy and not sacrifice."[7]

Night of the Soul

Another reason for us to hit a dry patch in our spiritual lives is when we enter the dark night of the soul.[8] In our journey with God, we may sometimes experience what John of the Cross described as the "dark night of the soul." This dark night will make us feel that we have hit a dead end on our journey. We find ourselves entering a dry patch and nothing seems to excite us anymore. We lose the passion and appetite for the things in the world and for the things of God. A sense of failure sinks in and to quit the inward journey becomes a temptation. The initial euphoria has subsided and it leaves behind a bitter taste. Peter Scazzero in *Emotionally Healthy Spirituality* writes what a "dark night" means:

> Our good feelings of God's presence evaporate. We feel the door of heaven has been shut as we pray. Darkness, helplessness, weariness, a sense of failure or defeat, barrenness, emptiness, dryness descend upon us. The Christian disciplines that have served us up to this time "no longer work." We can't see what God is doing and we see little visible fruit in our lives.[9]

John of the Cross explains that it is by divine appointment that we enter into the dark night for God is using this time out of sheer grace to do a divine work in us. It is not a time to be fretful. Rather,

---

7. Steere, Batten. eds. *The Very Thought of Thee*, 19.
8. This section of the dark night of the soul is taken from my book, *Being Human*, 52–53.
9. Scazzero, *Emotionally Healthy Spirituality*, 122–3.

it is a time for us to still the soul before God and wait patiently for the period to come to a close at God's own timing. Richard Foster comments that this dark night is like an operation that requires the patient to undergo anesthesia in order for the surgeon to perform the surgery successfully.[10]

What has happened is that we are going through a transitional period in our spiritual lives. Like all transitions, we find ourselves confused, disorientated, and lost. I remember when I was in Hong Kong using the subway for the first time. The place was crowded with people moving in all directions. Even though I could read the signs in front of me, I was momentarily disorientated by the crowd and by the unfamiliar place I was in. It took me a while to figure out where to go and what to do. The dark night is like that of the birth of a child. She has to leave the warmth and security of the mother's womb, transit through the dark birth canal before she exits into the bright world outside. Transitions should be welcomed because they are necessary for growth and progress. When we come out of the dark night, we will find that we are closer to the Kingdom of Heaven. John of the Cross, a sixteenth-century Carmelite friar and priest, has these encouraging words for those of us who find ourselves entering the dark night.

> Oh, then, spiritual soul, when you see your appetites darkened, your inclinations dry and constrained, your faculties incapacitated for any interior exercise, do not be afflicted; think of this as a grace, since God is freeing you from yourself and taking you from your own activity.[11]

The experience of the dark night is common to the saints of God according to the prophet Isaiah. He writes: "Who among you fears the Lord and obeys the word of his servant? Let him who walks in the dark, who has no light, trust in the name of the Lord and rely on his God" (Is 50:10). To Job, it was an experience that yielded positive results. He said,

---

10. Foster, *Celebration of Discipline*, 128.
11. John of the Cross. *The Collected Works of St. John of the Cross*, 365.

> If only I knew where to find him, if only I could go to his dwelling! . . . But if I go to the east, he is not there; if I go to the west, I do not find him . . . But he knows the way I take; when he has tested me, I will come forth as gold (Job 23:3,8,10).

A Spirit-filled Life

Only the Holy Spirit can rejuvenate our spiritual lives. "For I will pour out water," says the Lord, "on the thirsty land, and streams on the dry ground; I will pour out my Spirit on your offspring, and my blessing on your descendants" (Ps 44:3). A rejuvenated life is like a well-watered garden or a spring whose waters never fail (Is 58:11). When Jesus talked about streams of water flowing from within those who believe in him, he was referring to the Holy Spirit (John 7:38–9). Like the garden that is well-watered, the soul too needs the filling of the Spirit. When we become a believer, Christ dwells in us through his Spirit. A Christian needs the filling of the Spirit in order to develop a Christlike character and be equipped for service. "Do not get drunk with wine," Paul writes to the Ephesians, "but instead be filled with the Spirit" (Eph 5:18). How do we know that we are filled with the Spirit? Avery Willis Junior shares his experience in *Master Life: Developing a Rich Personal Relationship with the Master*:

> The most important manifestation of the filling of the Spirit in my life have been a deep awareness of the love and presence of God and an increased effectiveness in ministry. Over the years, the Holy Spirit has repeatedly filled me for each task of service. Whenever I have sinned, I have asked him to refill me, and he has done so. The filling of the Spirit energizes and empowers different gifts in different persons, but in every case the result brings glory to Jesus and attracts others to him.[12]

To understand the filling of the Holy Spirit in our lives we need to examine carefully the meaning of the phrase, "be filled" in

---

12. Willis, *Master LIfe*, 107.

Ephesians 5:18. First, it has a passive voice. This means that only God can fill us and we can do nothing on our part to have the filling. Second, it is in the present, continuous tense. That means that we are to be continually filled at any time. There is no fixed time or a special time for God to fill us. He wants to fill us all the time. Third, it is in the imperative mood. This means that it is not an option for Christians. All Christians are to be filled with the Spirit. The reality is that many Christians are not Spirit-filled and they remain weak spiritually.

Recognizing the Spirit's Presence

To be Spirit-filled, we need to recognize the presence of the Spirit in our lives.[13] The Spirit is present in those daily activities that move our hearts toward the desire to love and serve God and others more. In these activities, we are led by the Spirit (Gal 5:25). Conversely, the Spirit is absent from those activities that gratify the desires of the sinful nature. These activities will move our hearts away from loving and serving God and others. Instead of keeping in step with the Spirit we quench or grieve the Holy Spirit by our activities (Eph 4:30; 1 Thess 5:19). To live by the Spirit, we need to discern the movements of the Spirit in our hearts. Paul says the acts of the sinful nature are obvious to all (Gal 5:19). There is no reason why we cannot identify them. When we indulge in these activities we know that these will grieve the Spirit that dwells inside us. Our sensitivity to the Spirit's prompting in our hearts will prevent us from participating in these activities if we want to live the Spirit-filled life. Conversely, those activities that promote love, joy, peace, patience, kindness, goodness, faithfulness, gentleness, and self-control are led by the Spirit. Our response to the Spirit's movement in our lives is in our own hands. We have the choice to choose to be led by the Spirit or to quench his promptings.

The Spirit is a gentle Person and he does not speak in a loud voice. He speaks in a "still small voice" and unless we take time to

---

13. Hauser, *Moving in the Spirit*, 30.

notice it we will easily miss his voice speaking to us. The voice can be so faint that unless we have a vital and close relationship with him we may miss listening to his voice. Often we are too busy to hear the soft promptings of the Spirit in our lives. Whenever we feel a certain restraint, we need to stop moving any further for fear that we have quenched the Spirit without knowing it. Our sensitivity to the Spirit gradually loses its intensity if we dismiss such promptings and quench the Spirit time after time. It is easy for us to ignore the Spirit when our focus is on Christ or his Church. No wonder he is called the "forgotten" God. This should not be the case because Jesus sent the Spirit to continue with the work that he had begun on earth. Jesus said that it was better for him to go so that he could send the Holy Spirit to come to his disciples (John 16:7). The following prayer by the Eastern Church reveals this truth:

> Without the Holy Spirit, God is distant, Christ remains in the past, the Gospel is dead, the Church is just an organization, authority a domination, mission a propaganda, worship a ceremonial, and Christian way of life a servitude.[14]

We often find ourselves hitting a dry patch in our spiritual lives. This may due to burning out: exhaustion due to physical or emotional fatigue caused by many factors like too much stress in work, poor diet, lack of sleep or exercise. Unconfessed sin in our lives can also cause spiritual lethargy. We need to deal with these causes seriously if we want our lives to be rejuvenated. Spiritual dryness may not necessarily be bad for our souls if it is used by God to help us move on to the next level in our journey with him. We experience the "dark night" when our feelings for God evaporate into thin air and nothing excites us anymore. During this period of time we should not be fretful but patiently wait for the time to

---

14. Hauser, *Moving in the Spirit*, 24.

come to a closure. We will emerge out of this experience with a purer heart sustained by a steadfast and willing spirit.

All these happen to us with the aid of the Holy Spirit. Without him, our lives will not be rejuvenated. Our souls need the filling of the Holy Spirit. He will fill us when our hearts are pure and yielded to God. We know we are filled with the Spirit when our hearts are moved to love God and neighbor in our daily activities. To do these, we need to be sensitive to the promptings of the Spirit in our lives.

8

The Grateful Life

And be thankful. Let the word of Christ dwell in you richly as you teach
and admonish one another with all wisdom, as you sing psalms,
hymns and spiritual songs with gratitude in your hearts to God.
And whatever you do, whether in word or deed,
do it all in the name of the Lord Jesus,
giving thanks to God the Father through him

—Col 3:15–17

Grateful to the Maker

WE NORMALLY TAKE TREES for granted. Trees deserved to be taken seriously because of the role they play in our survival. We cannot exist without trees. We can exist without animals but not trees. Trees are the connecting link between the earth and the sun. We need the energy to continue living. That's the reason why we need to consume food a few times a day. All the energy we need comes from the sun by means of the trees. The fact that leaves are green in color is because leaves have chlorophyll. Chlorophyll is a photoreceptor that traps the light from the sun and uses the sun's energy to convert carbon dioxide and water into glucose or sugars which is food for the trees. The energy stored in the trees is passed down to us through our consumption of food. In other words, we owe our physical existence to the sun. We should be grateful that the sun never fails to rise at dawn every morning to greet us.

The Bible reminds us that our gratitude should go to God, the Father, who created the sun and the stars above us. If we are thankful for the sun then we should even be more thankful to the Maker for "every good and perfect gift is from above, coming down from the Father of the heavenly lights, who does not change like shifting shadows" (James 1:17). Unlike the heavenly bodies, the Maker of the heavens and earth cannot change. He faithfully "causes his sun to rise on the evil and the good, and sends rain on the righteous and the unrighteous" (Matt 5:45). Matthew Fox, a Dominican scholar turned Episcopal priest, writes about God's created order as a banquet for us to feast on:

> The Creator God has spread out for our delight a banquet that was twenty billion years in the making. A banquet of rivers and lakes, of rain and sunshine, or rich earth and of amazing flowers, of handsome trees and dancing fishes, of contemplative animals and of whistling winds, or dry and wet seasons, of cold and hot climates . . . and so are we, blessings ourselves, invited to the banquet.[1]

Ingratitude, according to the apostle Paul, is a serious sin. When people fail, in view of God's creation, to glorify him and to give him thanks, they are given over to indulge in the sinful desires of the flesh that leads to judgment and death. Paul writes:

> For although they knew God, they neither glorified him as God nor gave thanks to him, but their thinking became futile and their foolish hearts were darkened . . . Therefore God gave them over in the sinful desires of their hearts to sexual impurity for the degrading of their bodies . . . (Rom 1:21,24).

---

1. Fox, *Original Blessing*, 112–13. Cited by Thompson, *Soul Feast*, 123.

Two Great Gifts

The Gift of Creation

We are thankful to God for his goodness and love that endures forever (Ps 100:4–5). There are two great gifts that God has given to us out of his enduring love for us. The first is the gift of creation. God has prepared everything necessary for the first human pair to enjoy life on earth. The garden that God prepared for Adam and Eve was a good and perfect gift. It was a garden of delight filled with everything needed for nourishment and enjoyment. It was an enclosed garden of lush vegetation, flowing streams, and quiet tranquility. The first human pair enjoyed the simple pleasures of life provided by the trees, which were not only pleasing to the eyes but also good for food. The garden, apart from heaven, is the paradisaical image of human longing on earth. God invited them to his garden and played host to them. He sought to fellowship and communed with them.

Sadly, this communion between the human race and God was broken due to the grievous sin of ingratitude. Instead of receiving these bountiful gifts with thanksgiving and acknowledging God as the host, they tried to provide for themselves rather than receiving the provisions from God. They took over God's place and played host of their self-made universe. The first human pair listened to the sly words of the old serpent: "God knows that when you eat of it your eyes will be opened, and you will be like God, knowing good and evil" (Gen 3:5). It is a tragic denial of divine love.[2]

The Gift of Incarnation

The second is the gift of incarnation when Jesus came in the flesh and dwelt among us. It was a gift of divine love when God came to pay the price of sin on our behalf. Jesus entered enemy territory and came as a stranger. He came to his own and his own did not recognize him. At the Cross, our sins are forgiven and we are

---

2. Thompson, *Soul Feast*, 123.

reconciled and restored to be in communion with God again. This gift of eternal life is extended to us and we are grateful for receiving it. At the Last Supper with the disciples, Jesus played the host and the Lord's Supper was instituted. The Eucharist is celebrated to commemorate the redeeming work of Christ. The bread and wine which symbolize the broken body and shed blood of Christ point to his sacrifice at the Cross. He paid the full price for our sins so that we will not stand condemned before God (Rom 8:1). We are to receive the Lord's Supper with thankfulness in our hearts. Nouwen has this to say about the Eucharist:

> The Eucharist, which represents the departure meal of Jesus, is that sacred event that invites us to convert all that has happened in the past into one great wellspring of gratitude and then to move with growing freedom into our future.[3]

Forgetting God's Goodness

Thankfulness, as Lynne Baab says, is a way to take notice of God's specific works and the patterns of God's goodness in our lives.[4] Ingratitude will cause us to forget easily what God had done in our lives. The people of God can forget easily. Israel must not forget her past. She was enslaved and were aliens in Egypt. Now that she lived in the Promised Land, she must keep covenant with God in a relationship of dependence, faithfulness, obedience, and gratitude. They did not own the land, God did. They lived in the land with God's permission and grace and they were to be caretakers and stewards of God's land.[5] God reminded them that "this land must not be sold permanently, because the land is mine and you are but aliens and my tenants" (Lev 25:23). At the same time, they were to remember not to oppress a stranger or alien for they were once strangers in the land of Egypt (Exod 23:9).

---

3. Nouwen, "All is Grace" 41.
4. Baab, *Joy Together*, 23.
5. Pohl, *Making Room*, 27–28.

The prophets of the Old Testament were concerned that God's people would forget the mighty works of God as Creator and Redeemer. The Jewish festivals instituted by God were to help them remember God's mighty works. The Passover feast reminded Israel of God's deliverance of his people. The opening of the Red Sea allowed God's people to escape Egypt and from the clutches of Pharaoh. God did this work of salvation through a mighty miracle. Israel's amnesia led the prophet Isaiah to say these words: "You forget the Lord your Maker, who stretched out the heavens and laid the foundations of the earth . . . You have forgotten God your Savior; you have not remembered the Rock, your fortress" (Is 51:13; 17:10).

Deluded Idolatry

Ingratitude that led to Israel's amnesia had dire effects on the soul of the nation. Jeremiah had these words from the Lord for Israel: "But my people have forgotten me; they burn offerings to a delusion, they have stumbled in their ways, in the ancient roads, and have gone into bypaths, not the highway" (Jer 18:15; NRSV). We are surrounded by God's goodness and gifts if we care to notice them. The warm of the rising sun, breezy wind, birdsong, the laughter of children, food on the table, caring friends, beautiful flowers, an encouraging word, a warm smile, and many more should cause us to pause and give thanks to our Maker. Many of these things are free and valueless that money cannot purchase. Instead, we are distracted and deluded by the man-made "idols" of our lives. We live in a world of consumerism that constantly calls on us to "buy me, use me, taste me, love me, envy me, listen to me, follow me, and be like me." We are no longer satisfied and we envy what our neighbors have. We want more and better things. We work hard to get what we think will make us happy and satisfied. This will lead us down on a path of discontent and disillusionment. Jonathan Wells said it well:

> We have never had so much, yet we have never had so little. Churches are marching down the road of commercialism in droves, marketing Christ as a therapeutic product to meet all the self-centered, felt needs of consumer-oriented Americans. The spirituality is nothing more than self-idolatry and is in opposition to Christianity.[6]

Difficult to be Thankful

Why is it difficult for us to show gratitude? One day ten lepers came to see Jesus. Standing at a distance they called out in a loud voice to Jesus to have pity on them for they were lepers. Jesus saw them and told them to go and show themselves to the priests. As they were going, they were cleansed. Out of the ten who were healed of their leprosy, only one of them remembered to come back to thank Jesus for the cure. The rest, in their joy and exuberance over their healing, had forgotten to thank God for their deliverance. Jesus was disappointed when he noted that the only person who came back to thank him was a foreigner for he was a Samaritan.

Dependent on the Giver

When we show gratitude to the giver, we also admit our dependence on him or her. We celebrate our independence and do not want to rely on others for our own welfare. We rather take things into our own hands and chart our own destinies. We want to work or earn for the things that we receive. Humility is not one of our strong points. Pride prevents us to be grateful to God or to others. David Steindl-Rast, a Benedictine monk, in *Gratefulness, the Heart of Prayer*, writes:

> Why is it so difficult to acknowledge a gift as gift? Here is the reason. When I admit that something is a gift, I admit my dependence on the giver. This may not sound that

---

6. Cited in the article "The Christian Concept of Gratitude" http://www.doesgodexist.org/SepOct09/TheChristianConceptofGratitude.html

difficult, but there is something within us that bristles at the idea of dependence. We want to get along by ourselves. Yet a gift is something that we cannot simply give to ourselves—not as a gift, at any rate. I can buy the same thing or even something better. But it will not be a gift if I procure it for myself.[7]

To receive gifts from God, we need humility of heart. A story is told of some elders who came to Scete. The Abba John the Dwarf was among one of them. An old man came to give to each one a little cup of water to drink when they were having their meals. No one would want to take from the old man except John the Dwarf. They were surprised by John's action and questioned him later. How was it that he, the least among them, presumed to accept the services of this great man? John replied that when he gave people a drink of water he was happy that they took from him. So he decided to take the drink from the old man so that he might be rewarded and not feel sad that no one took the cup from him. The other elders were amazed by John's discretion.[8]

For Good Things Only

The second reason why we find it difficult to be grateful is that we can only thank God for the good things and not the bad. Paul does not agree with this because in his letter to the Ephesian Christians he calls on them to "always giving thanks to God the Father in everything" (Eph 5:20). Paul does not say that we can only be thankful when things are going well with us. He says that in everything, good or bad, we should be thankful to God the Father. Paul was in prison when he wrote this letter. His imprisonment should cause him to be ungrateful. We would expect Paul to be bitter or highly dissatisfied with the condition he was in. Yet, it was this spirit of thankfulness that helped to restore contentment and the joy of salvation in his soul.

---

7. Steindl-Rast, *Gratefulness, the Heart of Prayer*, 15.
8. Merton, *The Wisdom of the Desert*, 70.

We are familiar with the story of Daniel. King Darius issued a decree that anyone who prayed to any god or man during the next thirty days except to him would be thrown into the lions' den. This was bad news for Daniel. He knew that his enemies were there to trap him with this decree issued by the king. What would he do? Would he complain to his God concerning the king's edict and the dire situation he was in? Would he close the windows that faced Jerusalem when he prayed? Would he stop praying altogether at least for the next thirty days? This bad situation did not deter Daniel from doing what he was supposed to do. He went home to his upstairs room, opened the windows that faced Jerusalem, went down on his knees praying, and not forgetting to thank God as he had always done. Here was a man who, despite knowing that he would be sent to the lions' den, was able to give thanks to God at the darkest moment in his life. No matter how desperate the situation may be, we must not forget to give thanks for Paul tells the Philippians "not to be anxious about anything, but in everything, by prayer and petition, with thanksgiving, present your requests to God. And the peace of God, which transcends all understanding, will guard your hearts and minds in Christ Jesus" (4:6).

According to Nouwen, everything is grace.[9] We cannot be partial in our gratitude to God by remembering the good things and dismissing the bad ones. Of course, this is a natural response but this will not free us to move fully into the future. If we have not dealt with our painful past in a gracious way and still feel resentful and regret over what had happened then we are not free to move forward and bear fruit in the life before us. We need, as Nouwen reminds us, to gather all our past in gratitude so that it will become the source of energy that moves us forward with joy in service for God. We need to trust God that those bad moments in our lives were used by him not to punish but purify us so our hearts will be purer and our faith stronger. For these, we should be thankful. "Grateful people are those who can celebrate even the pains of life," Nouwen writes, "because they trust that when the harvest time

---

9. Nouwen, "All is Grace" 40.

comes the fruit will show that the pruning was not punishment but purification."[10]

It is easy to be thankful when things are going well with us. Our gratefulness will be tested when things go wrong with us. Will we be able to be thankful to God then? True gratitude lies in our ability to remain grateful even when we are faced with things that are not agreeable to us. "One act of thanksgiving when things go wrong with us," writes John of Avila, "is worth a thousand thanks when things are agreeable to our inclinations."[11]

Taking Things for Granted

The third reason why it is difficult for us to be grateful is that we tend to take things for granted. At times we are bewildered by God's goodness and gifts that we witness around us. The rays of sun that streak across the room when we open our eyes from sleep, the aromatic smell of coffee in the kitchen, the morning jog that fills our lungs with fresh air, the sweet smile of a sleeping baby in the cot, the kiss of our loved one before we head for work, the blue sky that greets us when we reach the top of a hill, and the hearty smiles of people we meet on the street. All these give us delight and we are thankful. Unfortunately, these things do not happen often. Most of the time, we stop noticing them when we get used to the routine of things.

The apartment I am staying faces the sea. Most of the people who come visiting for the first time are amazed at the beautiful sea scenery. That is their first remark when they enter the house. When I first bought the house, I was thankful to God for having such a place. I would spend time on the balcony watching the sea with its different moods and colors. I paid attention to the birds that flew over the waters to hunt for fish. The fishing boats that streaked across the bumpy waters and left a trail behind them caught my attention. I enjoyed the breeze caressing my face and

---

10. Nouwen, "Opening Our Hearts" 67.
11. Cited by Voskamp, *One Thousand Gifts*, 79.

body. I heard the barking of dogs when the call to worship from a nearby mosque was sounded. I also noticed the different types of boats and ships that streamed across the horizon in front of my house. After a while, I got used to the scenery. Routine set in and I stopped admiring the sea and the surroundings. Of course, once in a while, something like a rainbow that arches over the horizon catches my attention and I am once again reminded of God's goodness and gifts. But life goes on and I tend to take things for granted most of the time.

When we take things for granted we don't appreciate the things that are valuable to us. Only when these things are taken from us will we sense the loss and how much they mean to us in the first place. Take for example our mobility. We take for granted that we can walk anytime and anywhere. Only when we are bedridden due to an accident or a sickness do we appreciate the importance of having the mobility to move our bodies around. We lose our independence and need others to help us move even to the toilet to ease ourselves.

Benefits of Gratitude

Promotes Humility

Why is it necessary for us to cultivate a grateful heart? Gratitude will keep us from pride. It takes humility for us to be thankful for the gifts we receive from God. This will help us to nurture a good relationship with God for he opposes the proud but gives grace to the humble at heart (Prov 3:34). Which is why the primary place for us to express our gratitude to God is in our prayers. It is true that any acknowledgment of a gift received with appreciation establishes a bond that binds the recipient to the giver. When we thank God in our prayers, the bond between us will be enriched and strengthened. In normal circumstances, the receiving or offering of favors from or to others is a great way to nurture friendships.[12] As I am writing this paragraph, a colleague of mine

12. Baab, *Friending*, 131.

just entered my room and offered me a bag of fruit plucked from her garden. I received it with deep thankfulness and appreciation of her kindness. The bond between us is again manifested in this simple gesture of giving and receiving. I am already thinking in my mind how I should return back the favor in the near future.

Cultivates Contentment

Gratitude will help us to discover how much we already have. If we already have more than we need, why do we need to acquire more things in our lives? Gratitude is a way to keep us from the sin of covetous. What are we thankful for? We should be specific in naming the favors or gifts we receive from God or from others, whether big or small. We want to recognize the giver as well. In this way we can count the blessings and name them one by one. A grateful spirit leads to a satisfied and restful heart. Contentment sets in and replaces covetousness in our hearts. Contentment is a learned discipline and has to do with the manner we respond to the circumstances of life. It depends on God's providence rooted in his sufficiency and his strength given to us. In enables us to say like Paul that we "having nothing, and yet possessing everything" (2 Cor 6:10). It does not look to the circumstances of life but to a gracious and generous God who "did not spare his own Son, but gave him up for us all—how will he not also, along with him, graciously give us all things?" (Rom 8:32).

Changes Perception

Gratitude will change our perception of things around us. We usually look at life as either half-full or half-empty. We either are concerned with the things we do not have and feel dissatisfied or look at the things that we already have and be thankful for those things. Once, a man came to see a rabbi and complained about his situation at home. "Life is really unbearable. Nine of us are living in one room. What can I do?" he said. The rabbi answered the man saying, "Take a goat into the room with you." The man, on hearing this advice, objected strongly to the rabbi. The rabbi insisted that he followed his suggestion and asked him to come back one week later. A week later, the man came back and looking very tired and unhappy told the rabbi, "We are having a rough time with the goat. We cannot stand it anymore. It discharges an awful odor and is filthy." The rabbi again gave him this advice, "Go home and let the goat out of your room and come back a week later to see me." The following week, the man came to see the rabbi for the third time. This time he looked extremely please saying, "Life is good without the goat in the room. We are now enjoying the space with only nine of us in the room."

Induces Healthier Life

Gratitude not only keeps us from pride and covetousness, it also helps us to live a healthy lifestyle. Stephen Post, a doctor, shared in Guideposts magazine some data on those people who have benefited from a spirit of gratitude.[13] These are his findings: 1) Spend fifteen minutes a day focusing on things we are thankful for will increase our bodies' antibodies; 2) Grateful people are more focused mentally and less susceptible to clinical depression; 3) Those who enjoy a grateful mindset have healthier blood pressure and heart rate; 4) Grateful caregivers are better at caring than those less grateful ones; 5) Grateful recipients of donated organs heal faster than those who are less grateful.

God gave us two great gifts: the gifts of creation and incarnation. For these we are thankful. These two gifts demonstrate the love of God for us for the present time and throughout eternity. It is easy

---

13. Post, *Guideposts*, 78. Cited in the article "The Christian Concept of Gratitude" http://www.doesgodexist.org/Sep Oct09/TheChristianConceptof-Gratitude.html

for us, as a people of God, to forget the goodness of God working daily in our lives. Being grateful is a way for us to take notice of God's goodness in our lives. It also prevents us from being distracted and deluded by the many "idols" that entice us daily. Which was why God wanted Israel to remember by setting up memorial stones and enacting religious festivals like the Passover. Jesus instituted the Lord's Supper or Eucharist for the same reason. "Do this in remembrance of me," he instructed his disciples. In remembering the price that Jesus paid for us at the cross should motivate us not to look at sin casually.

It is not easy for us to be thankful. When we show gratitude we also admit our dependence on the Giver. This calls for humility on our part. Besides, it is difficult for us to be thankful for everything that happens to us. We can only be thankful for the good things and not the bad. We also take things for granted. We do not appreciate the good things that come to us from God which are mostly free. Being grateful has its benefits. It promotes humility and cultivates contentment in us. Gratitude also changes our perception of things around us. Instead of looking at life as half-empty, gratitude looks at the positive side of life. There is always a silver lining in every dark cloud. For this reason, a heart filled with gratefulness will enjoy a better and healthier life than the person who is afflicted with despair and depression.

9

The Delayed Life

Delaying gratification is a process of
scheduling the pain and pleasure of life
in such way as to enhance the pleasure
by meeting and experiencing the pain
first and getting it over with.
It is the only decent way to live.
—Scott Peck

We went on to heaven the long way round.
—Henry Thoreau

Difficulty in Waiting

MY FLIGHT WAS DELAYED and I could sense the impatience of the passengers waiting to board the plane. People kept going to the airline counter asking for the latest news about the delayed flight. The boarding time was delayed a few times and no one was happy with it. We were wondering what caused the delay. Was it the weather? Was the plane held up due to some mechanical faults? Was there a mix-up in the scheduling? Nobody seemed to have the precise answer to these concerns. We were kept waiting in the dark. The passengers' patience was wearing thin and the counter staff had a hard time explaining the cause of the delay. An impatient man started arguing and throwing insults at one of the counter staff. The poor lady had a hard time talking to the agitated person. Voices were raised to a high pitch on both sides. What could she do? The delay was out of her control. She was just an announcer of bad news for the airline. I realize that people are spending a lot of time waiting at the airports nowadays. The popularity of cheap air travel results in more waiting time for many travelers.

We may not like it but we do spend a lot of our time waiting. We wait for the queue to move, for the red light to turn green, for our turn to see the doctor, for the urgent call from abroad, for the traffic jam to clear, and for the meal to be served. Most of us do not like to wait and this may cause problems. Credit card debt is when we want to spend first and pay later. We buy on credit because we just cannot wait to save enough disposable income to buy the expensive watch or to go on an overseas tour. Couples who do not want to wait for marriage decide to cohabit instead. This may lead to some marital problems later. Some people, who have no patience, rush to their destination at high speed ignoring all the traffic regulations. Speeding is the main cause of accidents which can be avoided if all drivers keep to the speed limit. Most of us cannot wait but God can. We do not appreciate the value of waiting but God does. It is imperative, for the Christian, to wait on God. "Wait on the Lord," the psalmist prays, "and keep his way . . . Be still before the Lord and wait patiently for him" (Ps 37:34,7).

God's People Who Waited

There are many biblical examples of God's people who were called to wait. It is interesting to note that when God made a promise to a biblical figure, it did not mean that the path to fulfillment was direct and smooth. Often, the path took a detour and years of senseless delay before it reached its final destination. The delay might be puzzling but it was another step toward fulfillment. This happened to folks like Abraham, Moses, Joseph, David, Simeon, Paul, and scores of others. When Abraham was called by God with the promise that he would be the father of many nations, he thought that he would have a son soon. But God made him wait for twenty-five years before he had Isaac. Along the way, he made the mistake of going ahead of God's timing by having Ishmael first. Moses thought that he was the chosen one to liberate Israel from Egyptian rule. The timing was not right. He had to wait for another forty-years before God called on him to be the leader of his people. Joseph had to wait for fifteen years before his dreams were fulfilled. While waiting, he had to go through the anguish of betrayal, slavery, false accusation, and imprisonment. To Joseph, the period of waiting was part of God's plan of salvation for his family and the nation of Israel. When Joseph met with his brothers he had this to say to them:

> Do not be distressed and do not be angry with yourselves for selling me here, because it was to save lives that God sent me ahead of you . . . But God sent me ahead of you to preserve for you a remnant on earth and to save your lives by a great deliverance" (Gen 45:5,7).

Importance of Waiting

The parables of Jesus highlight the importance of waiting. According to the parable of the Ten Virgins, they waited for the bridegroom. Five came prepared with enough oil in their lamps to wait through the night. The other five came unprepared and the oil in their lamps ran out. When they went to get more oil, the bridegroom appeared and they missed his coming. In the parable of the Prodigal Son, the younger son asked for his share of the father's inheritance. He squandered away his wealth and before long he was impoverished. He came to his senses and decided to return home. All along the father waited for the son's return so that he could receive him back as his long lost son. In the parable of the Vineyard, the last batch of workers had to wait until the eleventh hour before they were recruited to work in the fields. When the time came to receive the wages, we would expect the last batch of workers to be paid less than the earlier batches. To the surprise of all, the last batch was paid the same amount as the first batch who spent the entire day working. In the parable of the Weeds, an enemy came in the night to sow weeds among the wheat in the field. When the servants discovered the weeds that grew alongside the wheat, they asked the owner whether he wanted them to pull the weeds out. The owner advised the servants against it but to wait for the harvest. The weeds would be collected first into bundles to be burned and then the wheat was gathered and stored in the barn.

Impatience Caused by Modernity

Why is it a challenge for us to wait? Most of us, by nature, are impatient people but modernity has exacerbated the problem for us. What is the common link among these inventions of modernity: the auto-teller machine, the car, and the supermarket? The common link is the word "convenience". The auto-teller machine gives us the convenience of ready cash without having to take a number and queue for our turn at the bank counter. The car gives us the convenience of easy and comfortable transport. We do not need to wait for the bus or taxi and subject ourselves to unfavorable weather conditions. The supermarket gives us the convenience of shopping for everything we need under one roof. We do not need to go to several places to get the things we want. These modern conveniences help us to save time and make us more impatient.

As we know, these conveniences break down from time to time and we become frustrated and our patience is tested to the limits. The auto-teller machine cannot dispense cash because our card gets corrupted or we momentarily forget the personal identification number. After a few tries, the machine deactivates our card. We cannot use the card unless we take the trouble to get help from the counter staff. Traffic jams become a daily occurrence and the convenience of travel is put to the test. Frustrated drivers tend to behave badly in a traffic situation and "road rage" is a modern disease that afflicts almost everyone. The joy of convenient shopping is cut short when we face the long queues at the cashiers' counters. The smart shopper will look for a few signs before she chooses to join a particular queue. She will look for the shortest line, the line with trolleys that are not packed to the brim, and the most efficient cashier at the end of the line. Even with these observations, there is no guarantee that the chosen line is the most efficient line.

The Patience of Trees

We all agree that patience is a virtue and it is good for us to cultivate this virtue in our lives. Nature is our best teacher. We can learn patience by observing the trees.[1] It is required for a young tree to grow slowly if it is to live longer. This slow growth is monitored by the mother tree which does not approve rapid growth for their young ones. The way to do this is through light deprivation. The mother tree shades their offsprings with enormous crowns that form a thick canopy over the forest floor. This only allows three percent of the sunlight to reach the forest floor which is captured by the offsprings' leaves. With this amount of sunlight, the young trees can only make enough sugars through photosynthesis to survive and keep their bodies from dying. Growth is reduced to a minimum. As far as the mother tree is concerned, this contributes to a good upbringing. As Peter Wohlleben, who worked for over twenty years as a forester, explains that a good upbringing is necessary for a long life. He writes:

> Scientists have determined that slow growth when the tree is young is prerequisite if a tree is to live to a ripe old age . . . Thanks to slow growth, their inner woody cells are tiny and contain almost no air. That makes the trees flexible and resistant to breaking in storms. Even more important is their heightened resistance to fungi, which have difficulty spreading through the tough little trunks.

1. Wohlleben, *The Hidden Life of Trees*, 31–32.

Injuries are no big deal for such trees, either, because they can easily compartmentalize the wounds—that is to say, close them up by growing bark over them—before any decay occurs.[2]

Patience Builds Character

There must be a good reason why the Lord wants us to wait and test our patience. Patience is necessary for us to develop character. "Perseverance," James said, "must finish its work so that you may be mature and complete, not lacking anything" (James 1:4). In other words, when we are undergoing trials while waiting on God, we must be patient and try not to get out of it prematurely. We must let patience and perseverance do their work so that we can become more mature and well-developed. There is a saying that goes like this: "When the student is ready, the teacher appears." When God wants us to wait, he is preparing us to face future challenges further down the road. The most basic and fundamental preparation is the maturing and strengthening of character that will help us to meet the tasks ahead of us. Without this, God cannot use us. A. B. Simpson, one of the 19th century's great preachers, wisely said this:

> God wants us to see results as we work for him, but his first concern is our growth. That's why he often withholds success until we have learned patience. The Lord teaches us this needed lesson through the blessed discipline of delay.

The Example of David

This blessed discipline of delay was applied to David. God was disappointed with King Saul, so he called on the prophet Samuel to anoint David as Israel's next king. But the kingship was not given to David immediately. He had to enter into Saul's service as his harpist. The battle with Goliath was a chance for David to prove

---

2. Wohlleben, *The Hidden Life of Trees*, 33.

his mettle. This victory over Goliath aroused Saul's jealousy when the women greeted the victors with joyful singing saying, "Saul has slain his thousands, and David his tens of thousands." Since then Saul schemed to have David killed. David had to flee from King Saul. He went to Achish, king of Gath seeking asylum. This didn't work well for David because they people were afraid of him. They remembered what he had done to the Philistine army. David feigned madness in order to escape from King Achish. David left Gath and escaped to the cave of Adullam where he was joined with four hundred distressed and discontented men. He became their leader.

Meanwhile, Saul kept pursuing after David and his men and gave him no rest. It was only after Saul's death that David was able to take concrete steps to claim his throne. This did not happen immediately. He was made king of Judah and settled in Hebron. The war between the house of David and Saul continued. David was able to become king over all Israel when Ishbosheth was killed in his own house by two assassins. All the tribes came to Hebron to anoint David to be their king. It took David fifteen years after his anointing to be king of Judah and another seven years before he could be king over Israel. David finally achieved success after more than two decades of waiting.

David's experience of waiting before the Lord was reflected in the psalms he penned: "Listen to my cry for help, my King and my God, for to you I pray" (Ps 5:2). "I wait for you, O Lord; you will answer, O Lord my God" (Ps 38:15). "Be still before the Lord and wait patiently for him; do not fret when men succeed in their ways, when they carry out their wicked schemes . . . Wait for the Lord and keep his way. He will exalt you to inherit the land; when the wicked are cut off, you will see it" (Ps 37:7, 34). "Wait for the Lord; be strong and take heart and wait for the Lord" (Ps 27:14).

Good for the Soul's Growth

Sue Monk Kidd recalled a time when she went to St. Meinrad Archabbey for a retreat. There she met a monk who sat perfectly still beneath a tree. She was attracted to his reverence and tranquil disposition. Indeed he was a picture of waiting. Later she had the opportunity to talk to him, "I saw you today sitting beneath the tree—just sitting there so still. How is it that you can wait so patiently in the moment? I can't seem to get used to the idea of doing nothing." The monk smiled and replied, "Well, there's the problem right there, young lady. You've brought into the cultural myth that when you're waiting you're doing nothing."[3]

The monk, placing his hands gently on her shoulders and looking straight into her eyes, said,

> I hope you'll hear what I'm about to tell you. I hope you'll hear it all the way down to your toes. When you're waiting, you're not doing nothing. You're doing the most important something there is. You're allowing your soul to grow up. If you can't be still and wait, you can't become what God created you to be.[4]

Benefits of Waiting

Yielding Control

How does waiting help us in our character development so that our souls can grow up? Waiting relinquishes our need to control the future or the ways God is working in our life situation. It is our concern for the future that we cannot wait. We rather make things happen than let things happen. To make things happen we are concern about the results. We need to set goals for the future and design plans to meet those goals. To let things happen we give up the need to control and let God take over our lives. It does not mean that we remain passive and not doing anything at all. We still work and plan ahead but we look to God and wait for him to provide the final results and directions for our lives.

Paul understood this when he wrote to the Corinthian Christians: "I planted the seed, Apollos watered it, but God made it grow.

---

3. Kidd, *When the Heart Waits*, 22.
4. Kidd, *When the Heart Waits*, 32.

So neither he who plants and the man who waters is anything, but only God, who makes things grow" (I Cor 3:6–7). In the parable of the Growing Seed, Jesus explained that a man scattered seed on the ground and left the seed to grow. He does not know how but the seed sprouts and grows on its own. The stalk grows first, then the head, and then the full kernel in the head. The sower has no control over the manner the seed grows. He only waits for the grain to ripen so that he can harvest it (Mark 4:26–29).

Recently I planted some blue butterfly pea seeds in a flower pot. I prepared the soil and carefully placed the seeds evenly in it. For several days nothing happened. I was getting impatient. At the same time, I could do nothing except to wait. I knew that given time and the right soil conditions, the seeds would sprout and grow. I had no control over when the seeds should sprout. My work is to prepare the soil and get it ready for planting. I could only water the soil over the next few days, making sure that there was sufficient moisture and not to soak the soil with too much water. My patience was finally paid off when tiny leaves began to emerge under the soil. Now the plants are growing happily in the flower pot.

Promotes Patience

Waiting not only takes away our need to control, it also develops patience, trust and hope in us as well. While waiting, we need to exercise patience. Jesus was on an urgent mission to Jairus' house to heal his daughter who was dying. The crowd was pressing behind him. A woman, with a blood disease, sneaked behind him and touched his cloak. She was healed instantly. Her bleeding stopped and she felt in her body that she was freed from her suffering. She thought nobody knew what had happened since she was part of the crowd that followed Jesus. Jesus stopped on his tracks and waited for the woman to explain her situation. It took some time for the woman to explain her medical condition to Jesus. Jesus was patient and did not hurry her. He waited for her to explain in detail what was her condition and why she came up to touch him. Jesus spoke not to embarrass her, but to minister to her needs. She was healed physically but she needed to be healed spiritually too. "Daughter," Jesus told her, "your faith has healed you. Go in peace."

We can imagine the impatience of the crowd around him when Jesus stopped and talked to the woman. The request was urgent. The girl was in critical condition and yet the rabbi took some time to talk to an unknown woman about her medical history! The impatience of the crowd was justified when some men coming from Jairus' house announced that his daughter had died and not to bother the teacher anymore. We can imagine the crowd's reaction to the bad news. Disappointment and blame were written on their facial expressions. Jesus ignored the crowd's reaction and proceeded to heal Jairus' daughter. We can see the contrast between the patience of Jesus and those of the crowd. Jesus was willing to wait to attend to a sick woman. The crowd was in a hurry to see a miracle performed by the rabbi.

Building Hope and Trust

Waiting also promotes hope and trust. When we wait for our friends to visit us, we wait with anticipation and hope. We also trust that they will keep the appointment and will not let us down. Of course, our friends can let us down from time to time. When we wait on God, things are different. God will not disappoint us for he is trustworthy and faithful in keeping his promises to us. That is the reason why the psalmist can say these words: "We wait in hope for the Lord for he is our help and our shield" (Ps 33:20). Micah the prophet was confident that God would hear his prayers to him. He spoke these words: "But as for me, I watch in hope for the Lord, I wait for God my Savior; my God will hear me" (Mic 7:7). Despite Israel's failings and God's judgment on her, the prophet Isaiah waited and trusted in his God. He said, "I will wait on the Lord, who is hiding his face from the house of Jacob. I will put my trust in him" (Is 8:17).

A Story of Waiting

Ha Jin's novel won the National Book Award for Fiction in 1999. The story revolves around three people: Lin Kong, a doctor working in an army hospital, his wife Shuyu, and Manna Wu, a nurse, who worked in the same hospital as Lin. Lin's marriage to Shuyu was arranged by his parents. Lin was away from home most of the time and Shuyu cared for their daughter and also Lin's aging parents. Shuyu's devotion and dedication to Lin and the family were unquestionable. Meanwhile, Lin developed an affection for Manna and decided to divorce his wife in order to marry her. The contrast between the two women was apparent. Shuyu was unsophisticated, illiterate and feudal. Manna, on the other hand, was charming, educated, and willful. Each year when he came home for the few days, he proposed to divorce Shuyu but was turned down by her. This happened for eighteen years. During this period of waiting, Manna was getting frustrated with Lin who apparently was not able to convince his wife to the divorce. They had to repress their desires publicly because of the sterile atmosphere at the hospital. They were not allowed to meet outside and their close relationship received suspicious glances and malicious gossips.

Finally, Lin was able to divorce his wife based on a law that allowed the divorce if the couple had been separated for eighteen years. Lin thought that he could now have the freedom to be with Manna. He was wrong. When Lin was with Manna, he found out that he no longer loved her. Shortly, Manna gave birth to a pair of twins. Lin was devastated when he knew of Manna's failing health. If she passed away he had to take care of their two children. It was during this time that Lin finally recognized how much he needed Shuyu to be at his side. He missed Shuyu's devotion, dedication, and care for him and the family. When Manna passed away, Lin went back home to meet up with Shuyu. He asked for her forgiveness and would like her to help take care of Manna's two children.

The story is about Lin waiting to divorce his wife in order to satisfy his own selfish desires. He waited for eighteen years and not without anguish, disappointment and unfulfilled desires. The story

THE DELAYED LIFE

ended with a peculiar twist. After eighteen long years of wanting to divorce his wife, Lin, in the end came back to her. In this regard, Lin's waiting was futile. He did not get what he wanted. In the end, he had to get Shuyu to care for his two children. In reality, the person who waited was Shuyu. She waited for eighteen long years for Lin to come back to her. Unlike Lin, she never wavered in what she hoped for. She remained dedicated and devoted to her role as a wife.

While we always think of ourselves waiting on God, it never dawned on us that God is patiently waiting for us as well. He waits for us to yield our control to him, to learn patience, and to put our hope and trust on him. He waits to see our character transformed and bearing fruit. He waits for us to get ready for his coming again. He waits for us to come back to him when we go astray and are on the wrong path. When Israel sinned, God waited for her to come back to him. "All day long," God says, "I have held out my hands to an obstinate people, who walk in ways not good . . ." (Is 65:2). The Lord longs to be gracious to those who wait on him. "Yet the Lord longs," Isaiah wrote, "to be gracious to you; he rises to show you compassion. For the Lord is a God of justice. Blessed are all who wait for him!" (Is 30:18). Yes, we are blessed when we wait on him.

We are so used to the modern conveniences that we find it difficult to wait longer than expected. Whether we like it or not, the truth is that we spend a lot of time waiting. Our lack of patience to wait can cause problems to ourselves and to others. Waiting is necessary for us to develop character and spiritual maturity. We see this happened in the lives of great men and women of faith in the Bible. A large part of their lives was spent waiting on the promises of God to be fulfilled. The teachings of Jesus, especially in the parables, advocate the importance of waiting. Jesus, himself, set the example of waiting on God. Jesus waited for 30 years before he could begin his ministry on earth. Meanwhile, he had to learn patience like any human person. If we lack patience, God cannot use us in a way he wants. The ability to wait is good for the soul. When we wait we learn to yield control of our lives to God, to develop patience, and to nurture hope and trust in him. While we always think of our waiting on God, it is good for us to know that God is also waiting for us as well. God waits for us to be transformed in character and spiritual maturity so that we can serve him well.

10

The Cross-bearing Christian

And anyone who does not carry his cross and follow me cannot be my disciple

—Luke 14:27

The Story of Yu Qing

THE OTHER DAY I was watching a documentary about a volunteer for Teach for China. Teach for China is a program that aims to recruit fresh graduates from top universities in the United States and China to teach in rural schools in China. The educational inequality between the poor rural schools and the better-off urban schools is unbelievable. Only less than 5 percent of the students in rural schools are college-bound whereas eighty percent of the students in urban schools will enter university after high school. The Teach for China program aims to address this problem of academic imbalance. The mindset behind this program is that the child's capacity to learn is not the fault of the child but is based on providing outside support. The rural child can do just as well if given the same opportunities as the urban child.

Yu Qing graduated from a university in Saint Louis in the United States. She joined the program and was assigned to teach in a primary school in Beihai county in Southern Gansu province. Gansu is one of the poorest provinces in China. When interviewed, Yu Qing said that she had no regrets in joining the program soon after her graduation. Coming from an urban, middle-class background she had to make major adjustments living in a rural setting. Previously she had a room to herself, but now she had to share with another colleague in a smaller dormitory. Many of her friends were doing well in their careers but she was never envious of them. Instead, she decided to take a different path based on her passion for teaching and love for rural children. Her parents who had supported her while studying overseas were not too keen for their daughter to begin her life career in this way. They at last relented when they visited their daughter and saw what she was doing in the school. Yu Qing was well loved by her students. Her English class was a favorite among the students. Her selfless contribution coupled with her warmth, simple personality inspired many people who got to know her.

I do not know whether Yu Qing is a Christian or not. What I do know from the interview in the documentary is that she put the interest of others before her own self-interest. She was willing to forgo her future prospects for her strong beliefs in addressing the issue of inequality in the poorest parts of China. In this way, she was like the seed that falls to the ground and dies and in doing so produce many more seeds (John 12:24). When asked by the interviewer whether her contribution would make an impact in the children's lives having spent only one year with them, she said, "When I leave, others will take over my place to teach the children. I just plant a seed in their lives and hopefully one day it will sprout and grow and their lives are changed forever." Yu Qing has set a good example for those of us who want to take heed to Jesus' words that call on us to deny ourselves and take up the cross and follow him (Mark 8:34).

Two Ways of Being

Cross-bearing Christians need to understand that there are two ways of being in the world.[1] Jeremiah wrote about the two ways of being:

> Cursed is the one who trusts in man, who depends on flesh for his strength and whose heart turns away from the Lord. He will be like a bush in the wastelands; . . . But blessed is the man who trusts in the Lord, whose confidence is in him. He will be like a tree planted by the water . . . The heart is deceitful all things and beyond cure. Who can understand it? (Jer 17:5-8).

The two ways of being are the two selves residing in us. The false self that trusts in its own flesh and strength and the true self that trusts in the Lord and whose confidence is in him. Jeremiah reminds us that due to the deceitfulness of our hearts, it is not easy for us to distinguish between these two selves. The first step towards cross-bearing is to identify these two selves. The self that we are most familiar with is the false self. This is the self that runs our lives without us knowing it all the time. When Paul says, "For what I want to do, I do not do, but what I hate I do," he is referring to the false self operating in him (Rom 7:15). In dealing with the false self we cannot deal primarily with what we can or cannot do. We need to go deeper. Repentance is not just saying sorry for the things we have done, but for the kind of person we are that do such things.[2] We need to starve the false self to death. When a person carries the cross he knows that he is going to a place of death and be crucified. "Whoever wants to save his life," Jesus says, "will lose it, but whoever loses his life for me and for the gospel will save it" (Mark 8:35).

---

1. Mulholland, Jr. *The Deeper Journey*, 22-23.
2. Mulholland, Jr. *The Deeper Journey*, 23.

The Rooted Life

The Homemade False Self[3]

Our sense of self and identity are self-constructed and nurtured from a young age. The false self is homemade. At a young age, we know instinctively that we can be happy if our fundamental needs are met. What are these needs? They are the needs for security and survival, esteem and affection, and power and control.[4]

A child's basic needs are for survival and security. When a child is hungry, he cries and wants milk to ease his hunger. The mother, sensing this need, readily supplies milk from her breast. She carries the baby close to her chest. The child, while sucking milk, stops crying when he feels the warmth and softness of the mother's breast. This not only eases his hunger pains but also gives him a feeling of security. For this reason, breast milk is far better than powdered milk for young babies. Besides having better nutrients, breast milk also gives better emotional support for the child.

His basic needs change when the child becomes a teenager. His need for survival and security has taken a backstage to the need for esteem and affection. At this stage of his life, he begins to show interest in his outward appearance (especially in front of the opposite sex) and is conscious of what he wears and how he styles his hair. He spends long moments in front of the mirror brushing up his appearance in order to look his best in front of his peers. His esteem is dependent on how his peers view him. He easily yields to peer-pressure wanting to be accepted and be popular. For this reason, he takes their counsel more seriously than his own parents. He begins to exert his independence from parental control and turns rebellious. He falls in love for the first time because he wants to be noticed and yearns for affection.

An adult's instinctive need is for power and control. Most adults, at this time, will work hard at their jobs in order to get a promotion. A higher position means a bigger income and more

---

3. Material in this section is taken from my previous book, *Being Human*, 14–15.

4. Indebted to Thomas Keating for this section on the "homemade self". See Keating, *The Human Condition*, 13–14.

power and control over the subordinates. A bigger salary means more spending power, financial stability, and a better grip on one's unpredictable life. It is not strange that career goals, at this stage of life, become a priority that take over much of his time, efforts and resources. Frustrations set in when he feels that his career is stagnating and prospects are dimming. He may be thinking of switching job or even a change of vocational direction at some point in his adult life. This is in order to get a fresh start with the hope that things may work out differently in his favor.

The Self is King

This homemade false self revolves around a self-centered universe. The self is king and any stimulus from the outside is rejected or welcomed based on whether it can make the self happy or sad. "What's there for me?" is the catchword. Ironically, this homemade, false self is programmed not for happiness but for misery. Our false sense of self is based on what we have or do. It is also based on what people think of us, act before us, or say about us. We get angry when people say unkind things to us or blame us for what we do. Our ego is dented and we feel rejected instead of being praised. Our self-esteem is hurt and we do not feel loved. When we lose our job we fear for our survival and future security. We wonder what people will think of us now that we cannot enjoy the things in life as before. People shy away from us for fear that we become a liability to them. We hate losing power and control over our lives. Unhappiness, as Basil Pennington observes, is "not being able to do something I want to do, have something I want to have, or concern about what others will think of me."[5] Listening to our own voice or to the voices of others instead of God will lead us to a false sense of self.

---

5. Pennington, *True Self/False Self*, 37. Cited by Benner, *The Gift of Being Yourself*, 85.

The Temptations of Jesus

Jesus was tempted in the wilderness. He was challenged to listen to his own voice, the voice of Satan or God's voice. The first temptation was to turn stone to bread. Jesus was hungry after fasting for forty days. If he listened to his hunger pangs, he would have yielded to Satan's suggestion to turn stone into bread. Instead, he listened to God's words and quoted Scripture by saying, "Man does not live on bread alone, but on every word that comes from the mouth of God" (Mark 4:4). The first temptation tested his sense of survival. The second temptation was to jump from a high tower. This time Satan used Scripture to entice Jesus since Jesus said that a man should live on the word of God. Satan quoted Psalm 91 saying that angels would protect him from getting hurt when he jumped down. This act appealed to Jesus' affection for this daredevil act would help him gain popularity overnight from the masses. Everybody loves a hero. Again Jesus listened to what God had to say. "Do not put the Lord your God to the test," Jesus quoted Scripture (Deut 6:16). The third temptation aimed at Jesus' sense of power. Satan promised to give him all the kingdoms of the world along with their splendor if he would bow down to him. This test was the most appealing to Jesus. Jesus could have the crown without the cross. One more time Jesus refused to listen to his own voice or the voice of the enemy. He appealed to Scripture and to God's voice by saying, "Away from me, Satan! For it is written: "Worship the Lord your God, and serve him only"" (Deut 6:13). If Jesus had yielded to these temptations, he would have given way to his false self.

Putting Off, Putting On

The false self that has turned its heart from God is set to fail. Jeremiah warns us that this false self or way of being in the world is "like a bush in the wastelands; he will not see prosperity when it comes. He will dwell in the parched places of the desert, in a salt land where no one lives" (Jer 17:6). Conversely, the true self or way of being in the world is set to succeed. It is like "a tree planted by the water that sends out its roots by the stream. It does not fear when heat comes; its leaves are always green. It has no worries in a year of drought and never fails to bear fruit" (Jer 17:8).

How can we starve the false self to death? It is not easy to deal with the false self. It has been with us for a long time and to get rid of it requires some drastic measures. If we are serious about denying self and carry the cross to follow Jesus, we can begin by detaching ourselves from those practices that the false self enjoys doing. Paul calls on us to take off the old self with its practices and put on the new self by attaching ourselves to God and growing in our knowledge of him (Col 3:9–10). In practical terms, we are to put to death whatever belongs to the earthly nature: sexual immorality, impurity, lust, evil desires, greed, which is idolatry . . . anger, rage, malice, slander, and filthy language (Col 3:5,8). On the other hand, we can put on compassion, kindness, humility, gentleness, and patience (Col 3:12). When we put to practice God's word we are also opening ourselves for him to do his divine work in our inner lives, in the wilderness of our souls.

The Call of the Desert

The call of the desert will come to those who are aroused by a lingering dissatisfaction with formal religion. Institutionalized Christianity makes golden calves out of God with the purpose of catering to the self-serving needs of its adherents. It is too sentimental, sanitized, sterile, and self-serving for cross-bearing Christians. We do well to take heed to the apostle John's warning calling on us to keep ourselves from idols (1 John 5:21). The feel-good spirituality of modern-day Christians does not take seriously the call of God to deny self, take up the cross, and follow Jesus. In fact, it caters to the self-actualization of Christians by a mix of pop psychology and theology. God is loved for the good things that he can provide. The suffering of the cross is absent from such a religion. It is replaced by a gospel that promises prosperity, peace, and well-being without paying the cost of discipleship. I am in total agreement with Belden Lane's comment when he said, "I don't really need a God who is solicitous of my every need, fawning for my attention, eager for nothing in the world so much as the fulfillment of my self-potential."[6]

Abandonment of Speech

When God, in his grace and mercy, leads us through the wilderness of our souls, he will lead us to a place of abandonment. This is the place of death for the false self. Sometimes, this abandonment is involuntary. We feel abandoned when we face some serious sickness or severe loss in our lives. We face the abandonment of speech. Like Hannah, we are so deeply wounded with grief that no words come out of our mouth. Job's friends sat with him for seven days and nights without saying a word to him because they saw how great his suffering was (Job 2:13). Language is often used as an agent of control. The false self is good at using words to manipulate, influence, and propagate. It is not surprising that silence can be painful and intolerable for many of us. Stephen Kurtz, a psychoanalyst writes:

> In renouncing speech . . . we yield up something fundamentally human—a central means for declaring and expressing our existence. It is a kind of annihilation. Viewed this way, silence is equated to death. To discover that our lives are "rooted in silence that is not death but life" one must first keep quiet.[7]

Abandonment of Self

We also face an abandonment of self in the desert. The desert ignores our presence totally. The false self does not want to be ignored or unrecognized by others. We are disturbed when we walk into a room and nobody takes notice of our presence. According to

---

6. Lane, *The Solace of Fierce Landscapes*, 53.
7. Kurtz, "Silence" 137.

The Cross-bearing Christian

Edward Abbey, noted author of *Desert Solitaire*, this is the desert's gift to us:

> The fine quality of these stones, these plants and animals, this desert landscape is the indifference manifest to our presence, our absence, our coming, our staying or our going. Whether we live or die, is a matter of absolute no concern whatsoever to the desert.[8]

When I watched the documentary about Yu Qing I also came across a twelve-year-old girl named Xuelian. The family is poor and has little income. Despite her age, she takes on adult responsibilities. She lives with her grandpa and great grandma. Both are ill and cannot do much work. Besides her homework, she has to do the housework like cleaning, washing, and cooking as well. She has to help her grandpa harvesting rapeseed in the fields. The rapeseed has to be cleaned, dried, and crushed to make oil. When asked about her parents, she was teary saying that they had abandoned her since she was very young. She has lived with her grandpa since she was two years old. Her greatest wish, for a twelve-year-old girl, is for her parents to come home and stay with her.

At times we feel abandoned by God. In the midst of sadness and grief we cry out to God and yet he is, like the desert, indifferent to our pain. We feel that our lives are stripped away. Life has become nothingness like the empty spaces in the desert. Out of this nothingness, the self abandons itself to God. Meister Eckhart, the German mystic and theologian, has these words to encourage us about abandonment:

> If you want to live and want your works to live, you must be dead to all things, and have become nothing. It is characteristic of creatures that they make something out of something, while it is characteristic of God that he makes something out of nothing. Therefore, if God is to make anything in you or with you, you must first have become nothing.[9]

---

8. Abbey, *Desert Solitaire*, 267.
9. Eckhart, "German Sermon 39" 296–97.

Abandonment of Neighbor

Next, we also face the abandonment of our neighbor. We tend to take the view of others seriously and are easily affected by what others think of us. In other words, we view ourselves through the lens of significant others in our lives. We cannot get this attention in the desert. The false self has no gallery to play on and there is no audience. All is emptiness in the desert and there is no one to applaud or criticize us. In the desert, we no longer care about how or what people think of us. We are free to be ourselves when we die to our neighbor. Abba Moses had learned to die to his neighbor.

A magistrate in the city was keen to meet Abba Moses for he heard that he was a devout person. He came to the desert with the aim to seek him. He asked to see the Father when he met the first person he came across. The man told the magistrate not to waste his time looking for the old monk for he would be disappointed. He quietly whispered to him that this Abba Moses was a fraud and a heretic. He was not what people said he was. He urged the magistrate not to search further but to return home. This new revelation deeply disappointed him. The magistrate returned home to his friends and relatives. He was keen to bring down the reputation of this monk before them. Then someone asked him to describe exactly the person he met in the desert. "Was he by chance a tall black man?" he asked. The magistrate replied in the affirmative. He was told that the man he spoke to was indeed the Abba Moses! The magistrate went away greatly edified.[10]

Desert Detours

We do not need to enter a literal desert to die to the false self. Instead, we can detour daily to a solitary place to pray in silence and solitude.[11] One day a monk asked Abba Moses for a word

---

10. Ward, trans. *The Sayings of the Desert Fathers*, 140.

11. To know more about the practice of solitude and silence, please read my book, *Garden of the Soul*, 78–81. There is also a chapter on solitude and silence in *Take Up Your Mat and Walk*, 89–102.

of wisdom. "Go and sit in your cell and your cell will teach you everything," he told him. The monk, when confined to a time of solitude and silence in the cell, would open a space in his heart for God to teach him the way of the desert. Sitting in solitude and silence has a way of wearing down our strong sense of self due to our attachment to things, people, and ideas. By detaching ourselves from the enticements of the earthly nature, we become attached to God. Blaise Pascal, a French mathematician and philosopher, once commented that all the unhappiness of people arises from one single fact: that they cannot stay quietly in their own room.[12]

Instead of a real desert, we can carve out a "desert" for ourselves.[13] The discipline of solitude and silence will help to create a wilderness in our souls. The interior desert mirrors the external desert with its harsh climate and emptiness. We can enter a "desert" voluntarily or involuntarily. When my wife was given the bad news that she had ovarian cancer we were speechless and numbed with shock. We were stunned and did not know how to respond to the bad news. It took us some time for reality to sink into our hearts. Our world collapsed like a pile of bricks. We were transported to a place of desolation. We felt abandoned by God and left alone in a vast, empty space. We had entered a desert involuntarily.

Structures Falling Apart

There is yet another way for us to enter a desert in our lives. The desert can be anywhere where the familiar structures of the world have fallen apart—a desolated place filled with despair and little hope. It is an empty wasteland, forsaken and ignored by the world, where few people want to go. And Aids hospital, a hospice for terminally ill patients, a mental asylum, a center for intellectually disabled children, a nursing home for the elderly and infirm, a counseling center for abused women and children, or a rehab center for drug addicts can become a desert for us. We learn to

---

12. Pascal, *Pensees*, 42.
13. The material in this section is taken from *Garden of the Soul*, 81–3.

embrace the pain and suffering of the residents and share the solidarity of abandonment and nothingness with them in these desolated places. If we do that, we have carved out a "desert" for ourselves without entering a physical desert.

Deserts Based on Personalities

We also face different kinds of desert in our lives. To James Houston, professor of spirituality at Regent College, each person with their personal stories will face a different kind of desert experience. For example, the perfectionist will face a desert of imperfection. God will expose her weakness and give her the humility to walk through her failures. The giver will face the desert of inadequacy. In times of trouble, he is hard-pressed to seek help from others and God. The doer will face the desert of uselessness. She finds herself to be going nowhere and powerless to solve the problem she faces. The idealist will confront a desert of ordinariness. He finds life routine, boring, and lacking creativity. A desert of flux and disorientation is given to the rigid person who is afraid of change. The fun-lover will be transported to a desert of pain and suffering to sober him down. The controller will face a desert of chaos and uncertainty. To the pleaser, the desert will challenge her to confront reality and stand up for the truth.[14]

Deserts on Aspects of Life

Any area of our life can be a potential desert. The emotional, bodily, economic, vocational, and social aspects of our lives will be at God's disposal to shape and mold us. We have our share of emotional deserts due to disappointments and expectations not met. Unfulfilled longings, memories of past hurts and abuses, and failed relationships can lead us to feel isolated and abandoned. It is difficult for us to share with others our pain and despair. Bodily deserts are caused by illness, accidents, and aging. The sudden loss

---

14. Houston, *The Heart's Desire*, 178.

of mobility will lead to a decline in the quality of life. We feel helpless and lonely when cut off from people and activities. Vocational deserts happen when we lose a job or when we have to stay in a job that we dislike deeply. We feel caged in by circumstances over which we have no control. We find ourselves adrift with no sense of direction or certainty in terms of our vocational goals. We also face economic deserts. The mountain of bills gets bigger and it is difficult to make ends meet. Faced with a financial crisis we do not know where or who to turn to. We become anxious in view of the accumulating debt. There are social deserts as well. Some of us keep changing friends and have not learned to hold on to a friendship for long. The friends that we have come to trust turn their backs against us when we need their help at a critical juncture of our lives. Sometimes, we feel isolated and lonely even when there are people around us.[15]

The True Self

When we starve the false self to death through abandonment, we are, at the same time, allowing the true self which is planted by God at the core of our being to emerge and take center stage in our lives. When we die to the false self, this life which is hidden with Christ in God will live forth in us (Col 3:3). Our minds are renewed and we begin to see things from God's angle and our values are shaped by God's Word. Like Paul, we can say, "I am crucified with Christ and I no longer live but Christ lives in me" (Gal 2:20). To live the crucified life we need to detach ourselves from the desires of the flesh and to attach ourselves to God and to grow in our knowledge of him. The false self will not die completely. It will, from time to time, raise its ugly head. It is a daily battle for us to "deny self and take up the cross." We need to be vigilant in order to live the crucified life.

What does this true self look like? Sue Monk Kidd, in *When the Heart Waits*, points out that the true self has an inner radiance

---

15. See Rensberger, "Desert Spaces" 8–10.

which she calls "delight". A joyful and positive outlook on life even in the midst of painful realities. The true self relates to God as Mother who "suffers and feels and waits in order to create, birth, and heal." In identifying with this image of God, the true self is filled with compassion and care for the "wounded, the broken, and the alienated—the motherless of this world." The true self deeply cares for the earth that God has created. She senses a deep connection with the things of the world around her. She develops a deep reverence and awe for the things that God has created. She feels pain and grief when the earth is injured through the reckless acts of greed. The true self is anchored at the present moment and attempts to live life to the full. It is not hindered by the dark past or the uncertain future. And lastly, it is an authentic life. "It is okay," writes Sue Monk Kidd, "not only to imagine who we truly are inside but to say who we are, welcome who we are, and even *be* who we are."[16]

We cannot have the true self by seeking after it. The true self cannot be sought outwardly based on what we can or cannot do. The true self will grow and develop when we pay close attention to our inner life with God. In chapter 2, I mentioned that in order to be rooted in Jesus we need to spend time and space in our hearts to cultivate a close relationship with God. Our lives need to be centered and rooted in God. We can only achieve this when we begin each day with solitude and silence before God.

The cross-bearing Christian has to deal with the two ways of being. They are the two selves living in us: the false and true selves. The false self is the homemade, self-constructed self that we have nurtured at a young age. Our need for security, affection, and control is from the false self. It dominates our life. In order for the true self to emerge, we need to let the false self die. This is not easy because the false self has been with us from an early age. In order to

---

16. Kidd, *When the Heart Waits*, 184–200.

The Cross-bearing Christian

starve the false self to death we need to begin in a practical way by detaching ourselves from those activities that belong to the flesh and attached ourselves to the things of God which call for acts of compassion, kindness, humility, gentleness, and patience.

The cross-bearing Christian will take heed to the call of the desert in the wilderness of our souls. This call is a call to the abandonment of speech, self, and neighbor. It is not necessary for us to enter a literal desert. The voluntary practice of solitude and silence will lead us through the wilderness of our souls. We can enter the desert voluntary or involuntary. We enter a desert involuntarily when we face loss or pain in our lives. A desert can be a place of brokenness and despair filled with little hope. When we attached ourselves to these places, we have voluntarily entered into a desert. Any area of our lives can be a potential desert as well. The emotional, bodily, economic, vocational, and social aspects of our lives can be used by God to strip us of our false selves in order for the true self to emerge. The false self will not die completely. It will, from time to time, rear its ugly head. We need to be vigilant and it is a daily battle "to deny self and take up the cross."

Questions for Personal Reflection and Group Discussion

Chapter 1: People Are Like Trees

1. How has your concept of trees changed after reading this chapter about the importance of trees to our lives? Why do people take the trees around them for granted?

2. What can you learn from trees that will help you to be better inhabitants of this earth? What are the ways you can co-exist with trees so that you can fulfill the call of God to be stewards of the good earth?

3. Do you think the tree metaphor used throughout this book provides good guidance in terms of your walk with God? If people are like trees, how then should you behave and conduct your life appropriately?

4. This chapter highlights the different aspects of the Christian life that need your attention. Are there weaknesses in your Christian life that need your attention right now? What are they and how do you intend to address them?

Chapter 2: The Rooted Life

1. Why is it important for you to be rooted in Jesus (Col 2:7)? Are there lessons you can learn from the roots of trees on this matter?

Questions for Reflection and Discussion

2. Is it possible for you to be busy serving God and yet neglect your inner life? Why is it difficult for you to pay close attention to your inner life?

3. Has your thirst for God led you to some desert-like experiences? What are some of these experiences that led you closer to God?

4. Suppose you want to be rooted in Jesus. What are some of the steps you can take for you to sink your roots in Jesus?

Chapter 3: The Communal Life

1. Jesus began his ministry by creating a community of followers. What lessons can you learn from him about the need of a communal life?

2. Why does prayer play a central role in community life? In what ways can the support of the community help you grow your prayer life?

3. What are the differences between a community group and a Christian community? What are the reasons for Christians to join a community? Do you think these reasons are valid?

4. What are the ways a Christian can contribute to developing a genuine community? In your opinion, what is needed in order to maintain a true community?

Chapter 4: The Sacrificial Life

1. Do you agree that Christians should live sacrificially? How much of our sacrificial living is inspired by the Cross? Are there other reasons that cause a Christian to live a sacrificial life?

2. One way to live sacrificially is to offer our bodies as instruments of righteousness. Think of some specific examples that

QUESTIONS FOR REFLECTION AND DISCUSSION

you can be used as instruments of righteousness. Is it necessary to live counter-culturally in order to live sacrificially?

3. True giving is sacrificial. "If it does not hurt us to give then we have not given enough." Do you agree with this statement? Why do Christians view giving more of a burden than a joy?

4. Serving can lead to burnout for Christians and especially for ministers of God. What are the causes of burnout in Christian service? How can you serve well by taking heed to these words, "To care and not to care."

Chapter 5: The Reviewed Life

1. Do you find difficulty embracing the past? What lessons can you learn from Augustine and Joseph in terms of going back to the past in order to move forward in your life?

2. Reviewing the past can cause you to be remorseful or nostalgic. How can you avoid these dangers? How can you remember the past in a new way?

3. Reviewing the past will help you develop a self-awareness or self-knowledge. Do you think you can tell your personal stories to someone you trust in order to know yourself better? What prevents you from revealing your past to someone else?

4. Have you tried journal writing as a spiritual discipline? In what ways journal writing can help you in your spiritual growth?

Chapter 6: The Abiding Life

1. Why is it important that you stay connected to Jesus? How can you stay connected? What is the difference between reading Scripture as a text and reading it as a love letter?

Questions for Reflection and Discussion

2. The practice of *Lectio Divina* or spiritual reading of Scripture is not a common practice among Christians today. Why is this so? What benefits can you derive from this discipline?

3. How can the discipline of solitude and silence play an important role in your prayer life? What did the desert monk mean when they gave this advice concerning prayer, "The chief task of the athlete is to enter into his heart"?

4. Can you identify some of the characteristics of fruitfulness in your life? Have you experienced pruning from God and how has that made your life more fruitful?

Chapter 7: The Rejuvenated Life

1. Have you gone through a dry patch in your spiritual life? Can you identify some causes why you experience spiritual dryness in your life?

2. Confession is the door to the spiritual healing of your soul. How has Psalm 51 taught you about the importance of confession in your spiritual life? Do you like the story told by the Sufi master? Why are you attracted to this story?

3. Some Christians encounter the "dark night" without knowing it. Have you encountered this phenomenon before? What was it like?

4. How can you live the Spirit-filled life? How do you know that you are Spirit-filled?

Chapter 8: The Grateful Life

1. Why is ingratitude a sin? Why should we thank God for the two great gifts of creation and incarnation?

2. Why is it important for you not to forget God's goodness? What are the steps you can take to address this?

Questions for Reflection and Discussion

3. Why should you be thankful to God at all times and in everything? Do you find it easy to thank God not only for the good things but also for the bad things that happen to your life?

4. How does gratitude change the way you perceive things around yourself? Explain why a thankful heart will lead to a healthier life?

Chapter 9: The Delayed Life

1. Why is it important for Christians to wait on God? Why are there so many biblical examples of God's people waiting on God in the Bible? Can you name some of them?

2. How has the discipline of waiting helped you in your spiritual life? What other benefits can you think of when waiting on God?

3. Why do people today find difficulty in waiting? Do you personally find it difficult to wait on God? If yes, what are the reasons?

4. What do you think of the story in Han Jin's novel? Have you ever thought of God waiting patiently for you as well? Does this thought surprise you? If so, why?

Chapter 10: The Cross-Bearing Life

1. What are the two ways of being? Why is it important for you to know them?

2. Can you identify with the homemade self as described in this chapter? How can you let this false self die in order for the true self to rule your life?

3. How does God lead you to a place of abandonment? Have you experienced this abandonment before? If yes, what was it like?

4. Why are denying self and taking up the cross a daily battle?

Bibliography

Abbey, Edward. *Desert Solitaire: A Season in the Wilderness.* New York: Ballantine, 1968.
Baab, Lynne M. *Friending: Real Relationships in a Virtual World.* Downers Grove, IL: IVP, 2011.
———. *Joy Together: Spiritual Practices for Your Congregation.* Louisville: Westminster John Knox, 2012.
Backstreet, Anne. "Meditations Divine and Moral" *The Works of Anne Backstreet.* Cambridge, MA: Belknap, 1967.
Barton, Ruth Haley. *Sacred Rhythms: Arranging Our Lives for Spiritual Transformation.* Downers Grove, IL: IVP, 2006.
Baxter, Richard. *The Saints' Everlasting Rest.* London: Epworth, 1962.
Benner, David G. *The Gift of Being Yourself.* Downers Grove, IL: IVP, 2004.
———. *Spirituality and the Awakening Self: The Sacred Journey of Transformation.* Grand Rapid, MI: Brazos, 2012.
Bonhoeffer, Dietrich. *Life Together.* London: SCM, 1970.
Buber, Martin. *Tales of the Hasidim, Early Masters.* New York: Schocken, 1947.
Calvin, John. *The Institutes of the Christian Religion.* Philadelphia: Westminster, 1960.
Campbell, Charlie; Baotou. *Time* (July 27, 2017). http://time.com/4851013/china-greening-kubuqi-desert-land-restoration/ (accessed May 12, 2017).
Chittister, Joan. *The Gift of Years.* Katonah, NY: BlueBridge, 2008.
———. *Wisdom Distilled from the Daily: Living the Rule of St. Benedict Today.* New York: HarperSanFrancisco, 1990.
Crabb, Larry. *Inside Out.* Colorado Springs: NavPress, 2007.
Eckhart, Meister. "German Sermon 39" in *Meister Eckhart: Teacher and Preacher.* Edited by Bernard McGinn. New York: Paulist, 1986.
Edwards, Jonathan. ed., *The Life and Diary of David Brainerd.* Chicago, IL: Moody, 1949.
Fenelon, Francois. "A Persevering Will to Pray," *Weavings* IV:2 (1989) 38.
Foster, Richard. *Celebration of Discipline.* San Francisco: Harper & Row, 1978.
———. *Freedom of Simplicity: Finding Harmony in a Complex World.* New York: HarperSanFrancisco, 2005.

BIBLIOGRAPHY

Gonzalez, Justo L. *The Story of Christianity: The Early Church to the Dawn of the Reformation (vol.1)*. New York: HarperOne, 1984.

Hauser, Richard J. *Moving in the Spirit: Becoming a Contemplative in Action*. New York: Paulist, 1986.

Holzkenner, Rochel. "Roots of Resilience" Chabad.org. http://www.chabad.org/parshah/article_cdo/aid/966742/jewish/Roots-of-Resilience.htm (accessed May 12, 2017).

Houston, James. *The Heart's Desire: A Guide to Personal Fulfillment*. Oxford: Lion, 1992.

Issler, Klaus. *Living into the Life of Jesus: The Formation of Christian Character*. Downers Grove, IL: IVP, 2012.

John of the Cross. *The Collected Works of St. John of the Cross*. Trans. Kieran Kavanaugh, Otilio Rodriguez. New York: Doubleday, 1964.

Kang, Joshua C. *Deep-Rooted in Christ: The Way of Transformation*. Downers Grove, IL: IVP, 2007.

Keating, Thomas. *The Human Condition: Contemplation and Transformation*. New York: Paulist, 1999.

Keller, Philip. *A Shepherd Looks at Psalm 23*. Grand Rapids, MI: Zondervan, 1970.

Kidd, Sue Monk. "The Story-Shaped Life" *Weavings* IV/1 (1989), 19–26.

———. *Where The Heart Waits: Spiritual Direction for Life's Sacred Questions*. New York: HarperOne, 2006.

Kurtz, Stephen. "Silence" *Commonweal*, March (1984), 137.

Lane, Belden. *Backpacking with the Saints: Wilderness Hiking as Spiritual Practice*. Oxford: Oxford University Press, 2015.

———. *Ravished by Beauty: The Surprising Legacy of Reformed Spirituality*. Oxford: University Press, 2011.

———. *The Solace of Fierce Landscapes: Exploring Mountain and Desert Spirituality*. Oxford: Oxford University Press, 1998.

———.. "The Tree as Giver of Life: A Metaphor in Pastoral Care." *Journal of Pastoral Care*. XLV/1 (Spring, 1991).

LaNoue, Dierdre. *The Spiritual Legacy of Henri Nouwen*. New York: Continuum, 2000.

Lewis, C. S. *Mere Christianity*. New York: Collier, Macmillan, 1960.

———. *The Pilgrim's Regress*. Grand Rapids, MI: Eerdmans, 1986.

MacDonald, Gordon. *Restoring Your Spiritual Passion*. Nashville, TN: Thomas Nelson, 1986.

Mah, Mark. *Being Human: The Desert Way of Spiritual Formation*. Eugene, OR: Resource, 2012.

———. *Garden of the Soul: Exploring Metaphorical Landscapes of Spirituality*. Eugene, OR: Wipf & Stock, 2014.

———. *Take Up Your Mat and Walk: Applying the Metaphor of Walking to the Spiritual Life*. Eugene, OR: Resource, 2016.

Maricle, Christopher. *Deeply Rooted: Knowing Self, Growing in God*. Nashville: Upper Room, 2016.

Merton, Thomas. "The Inner Experience: Infused Contemplation (V)," *Cistercian Studies Quarterly* 19 (1984): 76.

———. *The Wisdom of the Desert.* New York: New Directions, 1970.

Moore, Thomas. *A Life at Work: The Joy of Discovering What You Were Born to Do.* New York: Broadway, 2008.

Mulholland, M. Robert. *The Deeper Journey: The Spirituality of Discovering Your True Self.* Downers Grove, IL: IVP, 2006.

Norris, Kathleen. *Amazing Grace: A Vocabulary of Faith.* New York: Riverhead, 1998.

Nouwen, Henri. "All is Grace" *Weavings* VII/6 (1992), 38–41.

———. J. M. "Opening our Hearts" in *Henri Nouwen: Selected Writings.* Maryknoll, NY: Orbis, 1998.

———. *Reaching Out: The Three Movements of the Spiritual Life.* New York: Image, 1986

———. *The Way of the Heart.* New York: Seabury, 1981.

Palmer, Parker J. *A Hidden Wholeness: The Journey Toward An Undivided Life.* San Francisco, CA: Jossey-Bass, 2004.

Pascal, Blaise. *Pensees.* Translated by John Warrington. London: J. M. Dent, 1973.

Pennington, *True Self/False Self.* New York: Crossroad, 2000.

Peterson, Eugene H. *Christ Plays in Ten Thousand Places: A Conversation in Spiritual Theology.* Grand Rapids, MI: Eerdmans, 2005.

———. *A Long Obedience in the Same Direction: Spiritual Disciplines for Ordinary People.*

———. *Run with the Horses: The Quest for Life at its Best.* Downers Grove, IL: IVP, 2009.

———. *Subversive Spirituality.* Grand Rapids, MI: Eerdmans, 1997. Downers Grove, IL: IVP, 1980.

Pohl, Christine D. *Making Room: Recovering Hospitality as a Christian Tradition.* Grand Rapids, MI: Eerdmans, 1999

Popova, Maria. "Hermann Hesse on What Trees Teach Us About Belonging and Life" *Brain Pickings.* https://www.brainpickings.org/2012/09/21/hermann-hesse-trees/ (accessed May 12, 2017).

Post, Stephen. *Guideposts.* November (2007), 78.

Rensberger, David. "Deserted Spaces" *Weavings* 16/3 (2001) 6–13.

Rohr, Richard. *Falling Upward: A Spirituality for the Two Halves of Life.* See www.Illuman.org.

Sangster, Paul. *Doctor Sangster.* London: Epworth Press, 1962.

Scazzero, Peter. *Emotionally Healthy Spirituality.* Nashville, TN: Thomas Nelson, 2006.

Stam, Carl. CarlStam.org. http://www.carlstam.org/familyheritage/jbstam.html (assessed May 12, 2017)

Stassen, Glen Harold. "Kingdom of God" in *Dictionary of Christian Spirituality.* Editors: Glen G. Scorgie, Simon Chan, Gordon T. Smith, and James D. Smith. Grand Rapid, MI: Zondervan, 2011.

Bibliography

Steere Douglas V, Batten J. Minton. eds. *The Very Thought of Thee: Selections from the Devotional Writings of Bernard of Clairvaux,* Jeremy Taylor, and Evelyn Underhill. Nashville, TN: Upper Room, 1953.

Steindl-Rast. David. *Gratefulness: The Heart of Prayer.* New Jersey: Paulist, 1984.

Stott, John. *The Grace of Giving: Money and the Gospel.* Peabody, MA: Hendrickson, 2016.

——— *The Radical Disciple: Wholehearted Christian Living.* Nottingham: IVP, 2010.

———. *Romans: God's Good News for the World.* Downers Grove, IL: IVP, 1994.

Thompson, Marjorie E. *Soul Feast.* Louisville: Westminster John Knox, 1995.

Tozer, A. W. *The Root of the Righteous.* Harrisburg, PA: Christian Pubs, 1955.

Vanier, Jean. *Becoming Human.* Toronto, ON: Anansi, 1998.

Voskamp, Ann. *One Thousand Gifts: A Dare to Live Fully Right Where You Are.* Grand Rapids, MI: Zondervan, 2010.

Ward, Benedicta. trans. *Sayings of the Desert Fathers.* Kalamazoo, MI: Cistercian, 1975.

Whitmire, Catherine. *Plain Living: A Quaker Path to Simplicity.* Notre Dame, IN: Sorin, 2001.

Whitney, Donald S. *Spiritual Disciplines for the Christian Life.* Colorado Springs, CO: NavPress, 1991.

Willard, Dallas. *Renewing the Christian Mind: Essays, Interviews, and Talks.* New York: HarperOne, 2016.

Willis, Avery T. *Master Life: Developing a Rich Personal Relationship with the Master.* Nashville, TN: Broadman & Holman, 1998.

Wohlleben, Peter. *The Hidden Life of Trees: What They Feel, How They Communicate.* Vancouver: Greystone, 2016.

Wright, Wendy M. "Memories of Now" *Weavings* X/3 (1995), 6–13.

www.ingramcontent.com/pod-product-compliance
Lightning Source LLC
Chambersburg PA
CBHW050826160426
43192CB00010B/1919